nwaLiving.com™
Established 1997

Hall of FAME Edition

Details of Honor Inside

1997

Podcasts + LOUDENNET™
Hosting | Data | Domains .com

LoudenNet.com™;

a 13th Square.com™ Origin Story

by: ***Will G. Louden*** ™ *willglouden.com* ™, Founder

MANAfits.com™ More than Benefits. Manafits.

HattieStage.com™ a LoudenNet.com™ Affiliated Studio

LPMPL .com™

Life People Money People Life™

Aglmax.com™

Musatown.com™ A Royal Light House — Prosperity Smart City Limits Illuminated!

MotherLAN Made .NET™ Leadership Africa Network

Watch. Game. Learn. Plus+ wglplus.com™

PangeaSoul.com™

TurntSwag.com™ Your FinTech Wallet.

diyNovice.com™ Doing. Life. Your. Way!!

AfricanParliament.com™ UNITY: THE Road to Freedom.

Forecast Flex.com™ Financial Empowerment. By Store. By Region.

William Mandela™

PangeaSoul 13 '22 WORLD TOUR™

Afro GUARD .com™ Guarding the Peace.

DocuDrag.com™ Paperless Cloud Storage.

13thSquare.com™ Knowledge on Demand.

BoutitBanc.com™ FinTech

OmondiOnyango™ A Birth at Dawn. Rising Son.

EVErody.com™ GreenTech POWER

afroFXCOIN.com™ 1Market. 1People. Many Products. 1Coin.

MA™

BB™

Afro MOCHA .com™ By: Will G. Louden

Podcasts + LOUDENNET .com™ Hosting | Data | Domains

LatinLandMade.com™ Final Production: South America.

eyeblix.com™ Your Voice Worldwide.

willlouden.com™

MANAfits™ More than Benefits. Manafits.

EVerodyEnergy.com™ GreenTech. POWER

Bio187.com™ Be a Killa.

WGLDNS.com™

SWAYOutlet.com™

ReunionWealth.com™ Health • Capital • Unity

Willintl.com™ First: Enjoy the Journey!

raillix.com™

Xtrat Payments+.com™

TurntSwag™ Your FinTech Wallet.

a *13thSquare.com*™ published product; a **willintl.com**™ managed project.

First Published: 2026

Book / Media Type:

Paperback Color

Hardcover || Audio

eBook || Internet

Also available in these formats:
Paperback Color ISBN: 978-1-63762-450-0
Paperback B&W ISBN: NOT AVAILABLE
eBook Reader ISBN: 978-1-63762-451-7
Audio Book ISBN: NOT AVAILABLE
Edition: The Origin Story

The "*W*," signature logo is by:

***Will G. Louden*™**

willglouden.com™

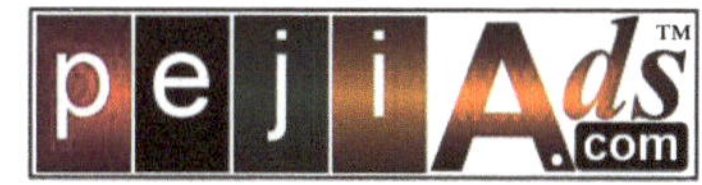

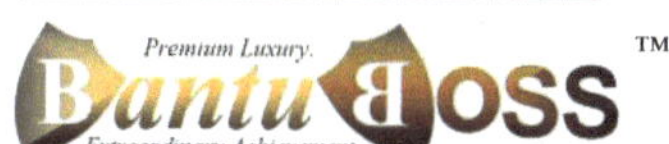

PangeaSoul.com™

***Will G. Louden*™** and/or sometimes: ***Will Louden*™** on 'select' popular social media platforms worldwide

a *13thSquare.com*™ Literary Catalog

by: ***Will G. Louden***™ (***willglouden.com***™)
Author / Founder: **WILLINTL.COM™**

LoudenNet.com™;
a *13thSquare.com*™
Origin Story

Paperback Color Version ISBN: 978-1-63762-450-0
eBook Version ISBN: 978-1-63762-451-7

By: ***Will G. Louden***™ (***willglouden.com***™),
Founder / President / CEO

For more information please visit: ***13thSquare.com***™

TOC – 2025 Invitation to Dialog Received from Forbes Books

SHOUTOUT *Forbes Books;*

Thank you for the *Invitation to "Conversation!!"*

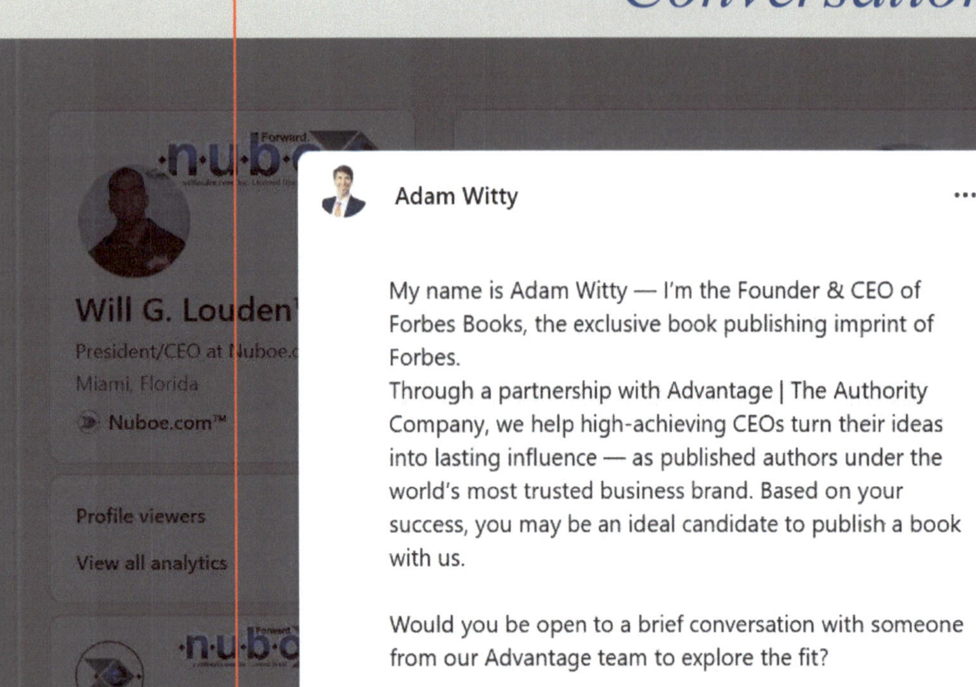

Although, we are in the process of developing our own publishing imprint, 13thSquare.com™, we are honored and grateful to receive invitations like this one received in November of 2025 to dialog.

We consider them both honors and milestones!!

Adam Witty

Founder & CEO of Advantage | The Authority Company, the exclusive publisher of Forbes Books, SXSW Books, Entrepreneur Books, and...

TOC – 2026 Pre-Approval Invitation to Worlds Largest Equity Free Accelerator

Will, You are invited to apply to Peachscore startup accelerator ..../Inbox

Alex Mojtahedi < @peachscore.co> Feb 20 at 9:02 PM
To: @willglouden.com Print Raw message

Hi Will,

I'm Alex Mojtahedi, Founder & CEO of Peachscore, known as the world's largest equity-free, data-driven startup accelerator, backed by the world's largest innovation platform, Plug and Play, an early-stage investor in Google, PayPal, Dropbox, and 30+ other unicorns. Since inception, we've supported over 1,400 startups from idea stage to growth across 100 countries, with our portfolio companies collectively raising $200M+ in funding. We also work in partnership with organizations such as the U.S. Federally funded Labs, Dealum, Carta, HubSpot, LMU, TCVN, TCA, and other leading institutions to support founders globally.

Each month, we open a limited number of spots as our team and platform identify promising founders and startups that align with our partners' thematic focus. Based on our review, your work stood out, and we'd like to invite you to apply to join the Peachscore accelerator. Peachscore is an equity-free, virtual, industry-agnostic, and global accelerator.

Honestly, being invited to join the (self described), "*world's largest*," startup accelerator excites us!!

Details are at the end of the book.

Hall of FAME

In April of 2026, we received a first ever international ***Hall of Fame*** Nomination. Details are found at the end of this book.

Hi Will,

We're excited to share that you've been pre-selected to apply to the Peachscore startup accelerator, recognized as the world's largest data-driven accelerator with 1,400+ portfolio companies from 100 countries that have collectively raised $200M+ in funding.

Each year, more than 1.6M startups apply to accelerators, yet fewer than 2% are accepted, leaving many strong founders underserved—despite history showing that companies like Dropbox and Airbnb were initially rejected.

To claim your spot, please sign up and complete the application at Peachscore.com (it takes under 4 minutes). As a pre-selected company, you are guaranteed acceptance into the current Cohort.

TOC – 2026 Who's Who in America Invite and Experian 700 Credit Score

Kristine McCarthy
Executive Vice President, Marquis Who's Who

Sponsored Mar 13

Invitation Enclosed!

Apply Today!

Hello Will,

We recently came across your profile and would like to invite you to apply for inclusion in the 2026 edition of Who's Who in America!

There is no cost or obligation to be included in Who's Who in America!

This is an Invitation- Only opportunity and inclusion is contingent upon verification and acceptance by the Marquis Submissions Department.

Marquis has been publishing the biographies of the world's most influential professionals since 1898. Inclusion is considered by many to be the pinnacle of success!

We hope you'll consider applying to be a part of this 125+ year long tradition!

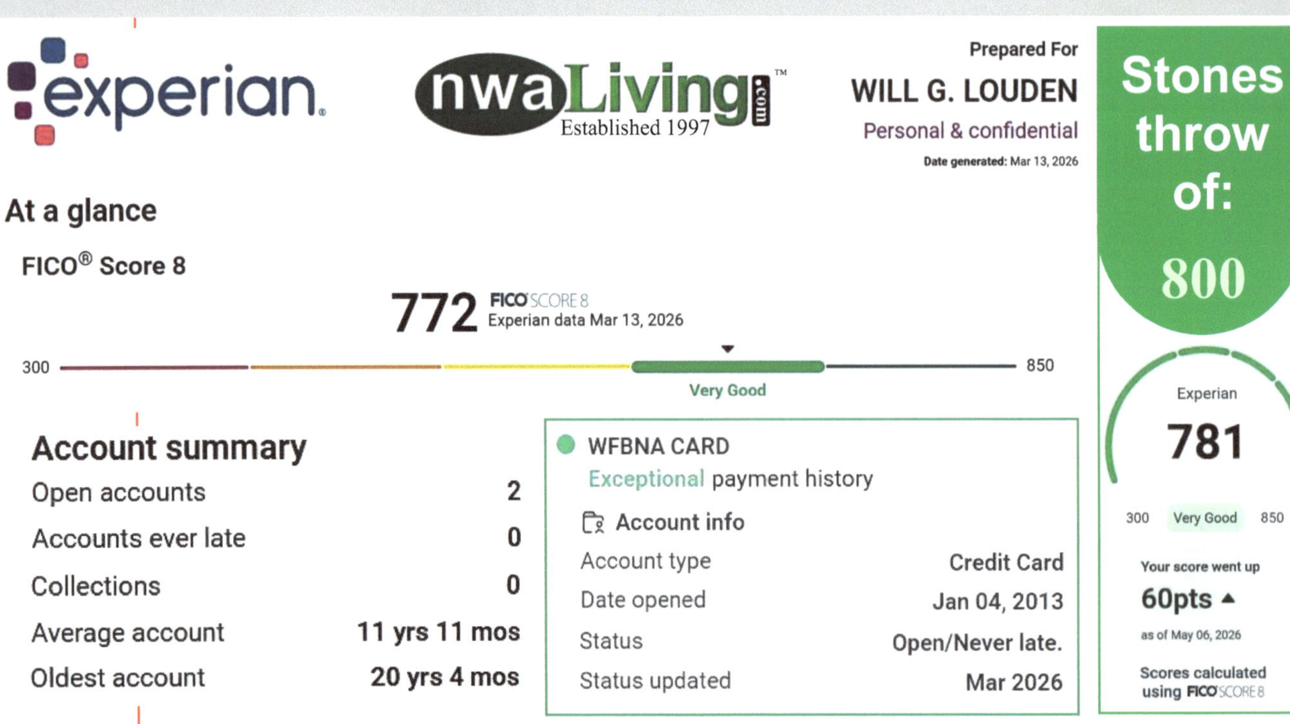

experian.

nwaLiving.com™ Established 1997

Prepared For
WILL G. LOUDEN
Personal & confidential
Date generated: Mar 13, 2026

Stones throw of: 800

At a glance

FICO® Score 8

772 FICO SCORE 8
Experian data Mar 13, 2026

300 — 850
Very Good

Account summary

Open accounts	2
Accounts ever late	0
Collections	0
Average account	11 yrs 11 mos
Oldest account	20 yrs 4 mos

WFBNA CARD
Exceptional payment history

Account info

Account type	Credit Card
Date opened	Jan 04, 2013
Status	Open/Never late.
Status updated	Mar 2026

Experian
781
300 Very Good 850
Your score went up
60pts ▲
as of May 06, 2026
Scores calculated using FICO SCORE 8

MANAfits.com
More than Benefits. Manafits.

HattieStage
.com

LPMdT
.com

Life
People
Money
People
Life

glmax.com

A Royal Light House
Musa
.com
Prosperity Smart City Limits Illuminated!

MotherLANDMade
NET
Leadership Africa Network
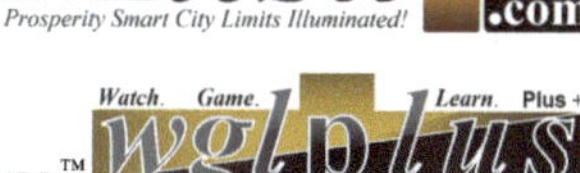
Watch. Game. Learn. Plus +
wglplus
.com

TurntSwag.com
Your FinTech Wallet.

AfricanParliament
.com
UNITY: THE Road to Freedom.

ForecastFlex
.com
Financial Empowerment. By Store. By Region.

William
Mandela

PangeaSoul
13
'22 WORLD TOUR

Afro
GUARD
.com
Guarding the Peace.

LOVE

DocuDrag.com
Paperless Cloud Storage

13thSquare.com
Knowledge on Demand.

A Birth at Dawn.
OmondiOnyango
Rising Son.

afroFXCOIN
.com
1Market. 1People. Many Products. 1Coin.

MA

MotherlandMade
.com .net .org

BB

Afro
MOCHA
.com

Podcasts +
LOUDENNET
Hosting | Data | Domains
.com

LatinLandMade
Final Production: South America
.com

eyeblix
.com
Your Voice Worldwide.

willouden.com

MANAfits
More than Benefits. Manafits.

EVerodyEnergy.com

Bio187.com
SWAYOutlet
.com

ReunionWealth
Health • Capital • Unity
.com $ ¢

LOVE

Willintl
.com
First: Enjoy the Journey!

RITE
2
RU
LE
.com

CarbonMonarch
Eye. Your. Crown.
.com
Royal Level Service: DELIVERED.

pejiAds
.com
Broad Range. Tremendous Reach.

Publishing.
13thS.com

bodaGIS.com
LOVE

lafamFX.com
One Market.

MotherlandMade
.org
Champions Aid Africa

MandyClan
.com
We. Are. One.

willouden.com

bodaGIStics
.com
LOVE

Financial Empowerment
FFX
By Store. By Region. By You.

CarMerMd
.com
Virtual Health Delivered

CrunkAi
Accelerated Innovation
.com

GordenAbson.com

lilYoungOne
Growing in Knowledge
.com

MMIntl
.com
Mother of: International Trade!

Willintl
.com
First: Enjoy the Journey!

LatinParliament
UNITY: THE Road to Freedom.
.com

OkeOga
.com

Phones • Apps • Safety
.com
Who's Calling You?

Forward.
n·u·b·o·x·e
.com

afroFX.com
One Market.

Beamoe
Text. Voice. Email. +
.com

raillix
.com

trat
Payments+
.com

ICONSean.com

TurntSwag
Your FinTech Wallet.

From the Root to the WORLD:
hoorooTu
HoorooTu Country Manager

SeeTHREAT
.com
Mitigating: Risk of Loss.

MotherlandMade.com
Final Production: Africa

Pre Seed;

a ***13thSquare.com***™ Partnership Agreement | by: ***Will G. Louden***, CEO

This book, **LoudenNet.com**™; a ***13thSquare.com***™ Origin Story, is about some of the most pivotal moments from 1997 to 2026, which helped contribute to our growth and whom we ultimately became.

This book was written by the firm founder, ***Will G. Louden***™ (***willglouden.com***™), who is a, Little Rock, Arkansas, USA, native and avid world traveler.

Thank you for visiting and we hope you enjoy our journey.

Project Dedication – 2026 diyNovice.com Student Developer Team

This book is dedicated to our Spring 2026 NJIT Capstone Student Developer TEAM!

BRAVO!

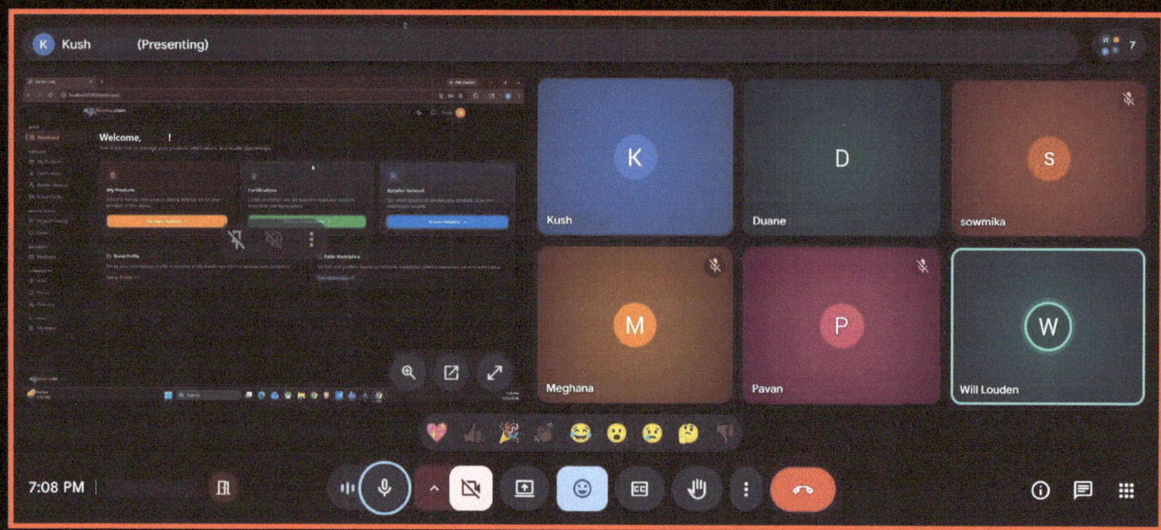

For more information please visit: ***13thSquare.com***™

Chapter 1 ('97 to '05)

Origin Milestones

(1) 1997 VGIS Started (as Virtual GraphX; Mentor Dr. N. William, RIP)

(2) 1998 Northwest Arkansas Living™ Magazine Started; nwahotspots.com™ nwaliving.com™; nwacafe.com™

(3) 2000 GoopyGrape.com™ Sponsor: Harps Food Stores) Healthy Kid Coloring Book and Tee Shirt Successful Launch at the Annual Harps Holiday Show

(4) 2005 ***University of Arkansas*** Graduate

Ch 1 – 1997 VGIS Started

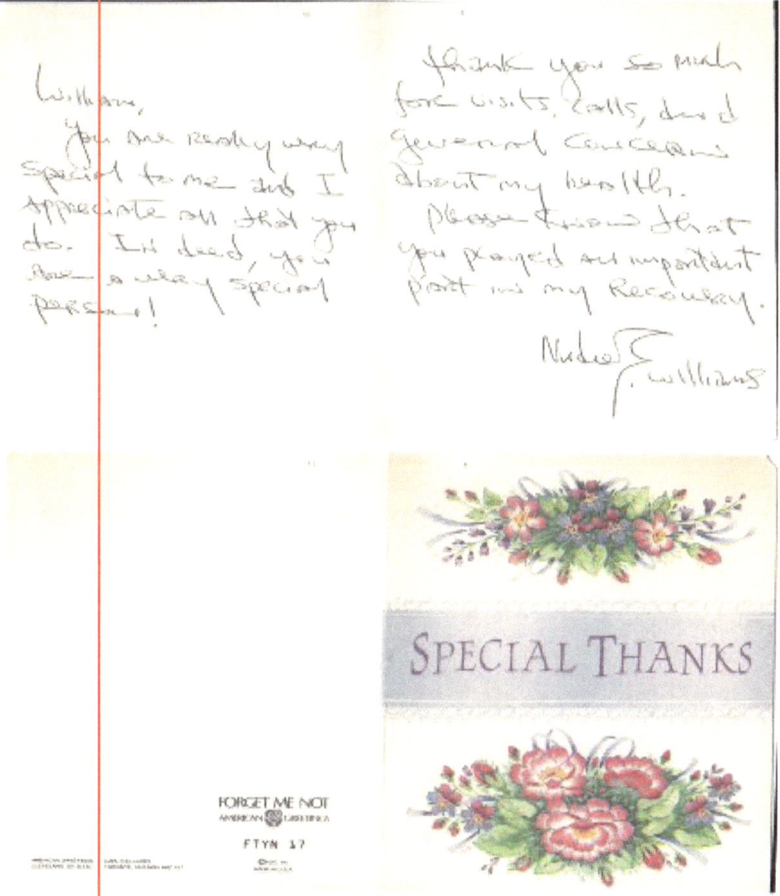

William,
You are really very special to me and I appreciate all that you do. Indeed, you are a very special person!

Thank you so much for visits, calls, and general concerns about my health.
Please know that you played an important part in my recovery.

Nudie E. Williams

SPECIAL THANKS

FORGET ME NOT
AMERICAN GREETINGS
FTYN 17

In 1997, VGIS was born, AKA ***Virtual GraphX***, Inc. When I started **VGIS,** I asked my then mentor, University of Arkansas history professor, Dr. Nudie Eugene Williams, to stand in as its initial chairman; this was done partly to teach me (I wanted to watch a pro in action) and to also make sure that things back then were done right.

As an honor for his mentorship, I stood by his side during his final days on Earth. Priceless.

Ch 1 – 1998 Northwest Arkansas Living™ Magazine Started

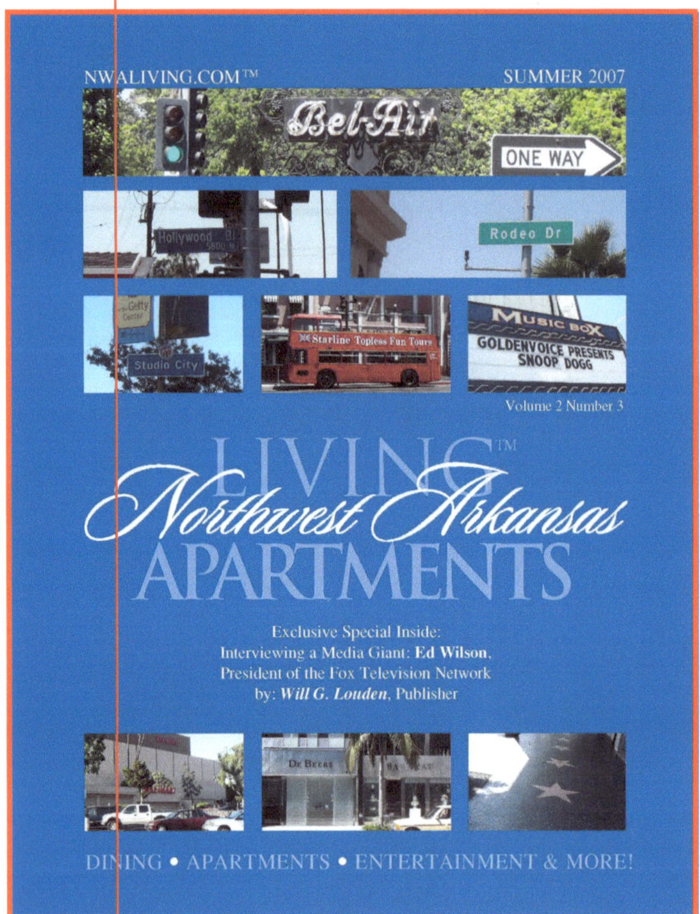

In 2007, one of the most successful publication projects that we ever engaged in, under the VGIS (predecessor) enterprise, played host to a truly significant interview milestone; it was with the then president of the FOX Television Network…

After thirteen years of prime production, the Northwest Arkansas Living™, magazine ended print production with this particular final issue and what a high note to end on… The trip out to LA, to interview the president of FOX, was not only a milestone, but it was also a, "legendary," dream come true!!

Ch 1 – 1998 nwahotspots.com™, nwaliving.com™ and nwacafe.com Started

In 1998, we also leaped into Information technology with the start of several highly successful regional Internet systems and platforms. These platforms were operated by and through the former VGIS enterprise. These technologies helped to shape and perfect many of the foundation stones that remain under employment by and through our vast ecosystem, even to this day!

The **Nuboe.com**™ Origin Story.

nwahotspots™

Established 1997 .com

Although the previous Internet system and portal, nwaliving.com™, was the third, or fourth, site that we ever launched, it's most certainly, by far, one of the most successful and longest lasting projects, that has helped us reach today!!

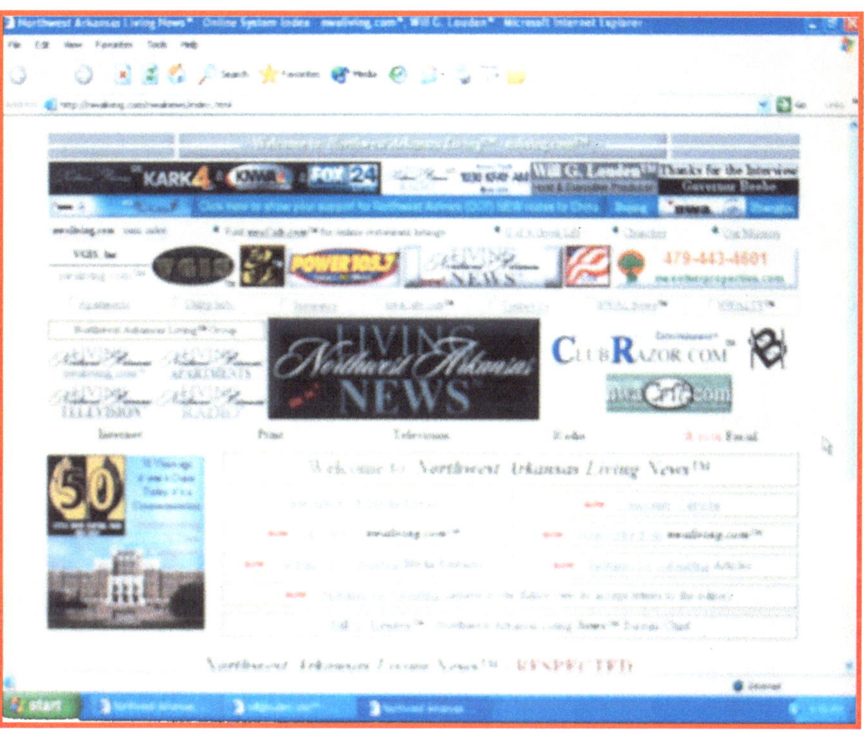

Agreement for Advertising Services:

Payment Terms: 5/10, net 30

Section Requested: ____________ Ad Size: ________
Ad Cost: ____________ Layout fees: ____________
Payment Method: ______________________
Bill To: ______________ DBA: ____________
Contact: ______________________
Phone: ______________ Fax: ____________
Email: ______________ Web: ____________
Authorized Signature: ______________________
Billing: ______________________
City: ______________ State: ____ Zip: ________

Design/Services (please check a box)

__ I want the Mullikin Agency to produce my ad
__ I will be providing my artwork via email
__ I will be sending my artwork via disc
__ I will be sending my artwork via postal mail

Publication & Internet Advertising Rates:

Coupons
Coupon: $150 Cash
All Ads are Full Color – CMYK (4 Color Process)

Other Ad's

1/8th Page:	$250
1/4th Page:	$350
1 Half Page:	$500
Full Page:	$700

Contact us today:
The Mullikin Agency
6200 West Sunset
Springdale, AR 72762
Email: @mullikinad.com
Subject line: VGIS Living™ AR Zoned Edition

Facts:
- 10,000 Copies
- White Vellum
- Saddle-stitched
- 4 Color process
- 40 Total pages
- Online as well

Publication coupons: W (3.563") X H (2.25")
Internet coupons: W (480 Pixels) X H (200 Pixels)

nwaliving.com™ – Sample Online Coupon (actual online coupons are bigger)

Mexican Pizza $.99 Plus Tax
SAMPLE
Open Late!
Northwest Arkansas Living: nwaliving.com - online coupon

All publication advertisers will receive 4 online banner ads. Coupons and online ads will run for 6-months minimum online @ **vgisLiving.com™**. An affiliated **vgis.net™** & **nwaliving.com™** system.

Sample Online Ads

This is a "**B4**" size or Center Square ad. This size ad usually loads in very prominent locations within our online systems for maximum exposure. The size of this ad is 190X190 pixels.

BENCHMARK REAL ESTATE, INC.
479.770.4300
the standard for excellence
• residential • farms • acreage • commercial • buy • lease

Online System

The "***Quad Select***" – system uses revolutionary technologies where we are now able to track total page views/impressions per banner as well as actual banner ad click-throughs. This system will enable our firm to help advertisers "stop the guessing" in online advertising and deliver measurable, sustainable and real results.

Our rotating banner ad systems load from secure databases, which select banners at random with a predetermined weight out of every 100 page views which is heavily reliant upon the amount of exposure which each advertiser has requested, and what size ad they have purchased, etc.

The Basic Group 479-751-8868
• Basic Construction • Basic Block • General Trucking

This is a "**B1**" size or Thumb Nail ad. This size ad loads throughout the text & body of our online systems. The size of this ad is 190X65 pixels.

B2 sized ads are animated.

BRAND NEW! ChapelRidge APARTMENTS

This is a "**B2**" size or Header ad. This size ad loads at the top of a page in the header file. The size of this ad is 219X47 pixels.

Wireless HookUp
Bentonville (479) 254-1967
Fayetteville (479) 695-1177
dish NETWORK
ESPN HD
HBO HDTV
HDNet
Discovery HD
SHO HDTV
DISH NETWORK HD PAK $9.99
*Some restrictions may apply.

This is a "**B3**" size or Anchor ad. This size ad loads either at the top, bottom or center of a page. The size of this ad is 600X75 pixels.

In the earliest days of our origin, we enjoyed a significant number of incredibly lucrative collaborations, including (but not limited to): large scale regional advertising agency partnerships, educational and institutional sponsorships, and even key major networked television and radio station affiliations and alliances, as well. These were golden years!!

Back then countless people and organizations helped to propel us to significant stardom. The image to the left is one example of a former multi-platform / medium, etc., advertising sales brochure.

During our THIRTEEN year reign in Northwest Arkansas, we achieved several notable accomplishments including (but not limited to), operating one of the regions largest online apartment locator and restaurant services.

Another extremely successful project that we produced, for a limited time, was the Goopy Grape™ healthy children's coloring book, online trivia contest, and project tee-shirt.

This project was produced in the year of 2000, in collaboration / sponsorship with the annual Harps Food Stores, regional holiday show. All items from this project were a smash hit with the children and families. Harps leadership liked it too.

Ch 1 – 2005 *University of Arkansas* Graguate

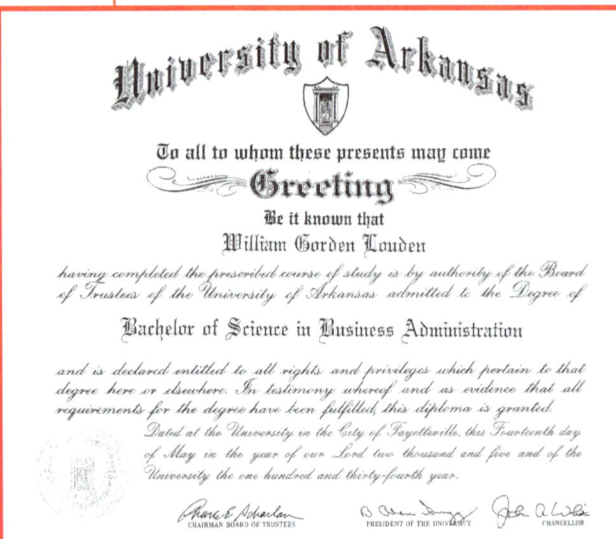

University of Arkansas

To all to whom these presents may come

Greeting

Be it known that

William Gorden Louden

having completed the prescribed course of study is by authority of the Board of Trustees of the University of Arkansas admitted to the Degree of

Bachelor of Science in Business Administration

and is declared entitled to all rights and privileges which pertain to that degree here or elsewhere. In testimony whereof and as evidence that all requirements for the degree have been fulfilled, this diploma is granted.

Dated at the University in the City of Fayetteville, this Fourteenth day of May in the year of our Lord two thousand and five and of the University the one hundred and thirty-fourth year.

CHAIRMAN BOARD OF TRUSTEES | PRESIDENT OF THE UNIVERSITY | CHANCELLOR

Perhaps one of the more encouraging times in our history was when we graduated (the founder) from THE University of Arkansas, Fayetteville, Arkansas, USA, main campus.

A lot was accomplished and reached back then. Knowledge, key contacts and connections were also established during these foundation years, all while: up. on. 'The. Hill!'

A few additional action items and/or accomplishments of note, by: ***Will G. Louden™***, while at THE U of A, off and on, include:

Pledging a fraternity | Becoming an RA (Resident Assistant) | Receiving an, 'All Student Judicial Board,' appointment (Chair) | Associated Student Government Representative | Arkansas Student Union Governing Board Member

Also, while at the University of Arkansas, as a freshman, we participated in and completed the, "***Emerging Leaders***," program.

Clearly, that whole experience set the stage for some really awesome things to come which would certainly help to contribute to who and what is now known today as: LoudenNet.com.

UNIVERSITY of ARKANSAS

Office of the Vice Chancellor for Student Services

427 Administration Building
Fayetteville, Arkansas 72701
(501) 575-5007
(501) 575-7575 (FAX)

September 7, 1994

Mr. William Louden
P. O. Box 2226
Fayetteville AR 72702

Dear William:

You are cordially invited to be our guest at a buffet dinner at the Chancellor's home on **Tuesday, September 20, 1994** from **5:30 to 7:30 p.m.** Dress will be casual. A map with directions to the Chancellor's home is included with this invitation.

During the evening, we will get better acquainted and will take a few minutes to have an informal discussion about students' interests and about the University in general.

Please let us know NO LATER than **Thursday, September 15th** whether or not you will be able to attend. Call Lisa at 575-5007 or stop by the office to RSVP. We look forward to seeing you on September 20th!

Sincerely,

Daniel E. Ferritor
Chancellor

Lyle A. Gohn
Vice Chancellor for Student Services

LAG:lb
Enclosure

The University of Arkansas is an equal opportunity/affirmative action institution.

In addition to being invited to THE, "chancellor's home," we also received multiple opportunities to meet privately with multiple U of A system presidents (post graduation), and in different years. This is simply – Spectacular!

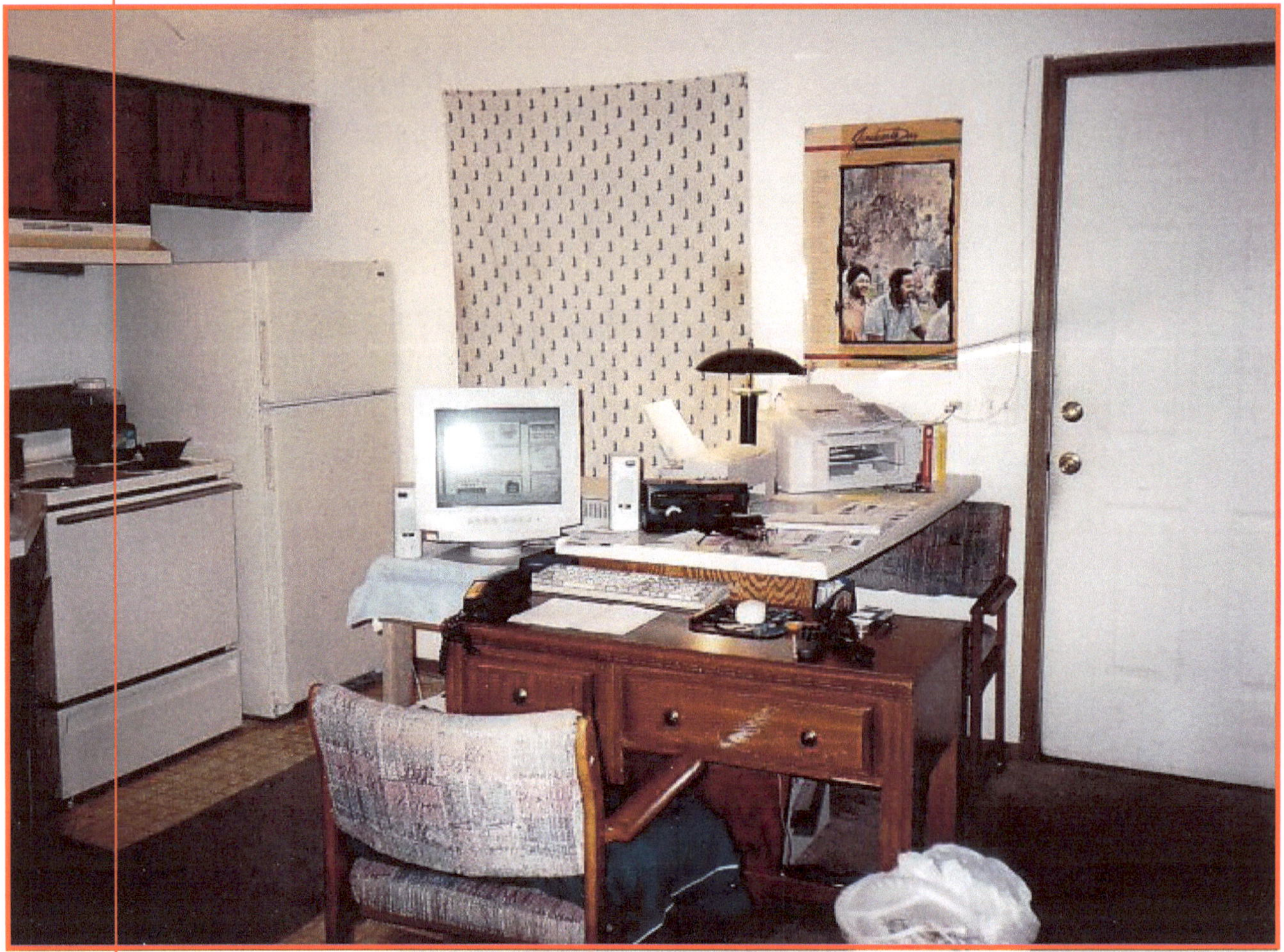

The real starting point and / or a point of, "origin," for the VGIS or Virtual GraphX, Inc. / VGIS DOT NET, Inc., etc. venture was this initial studio apartment, located on Holly Street, in the city of Fayetteville, Arkansas, USA.

ACTIVE

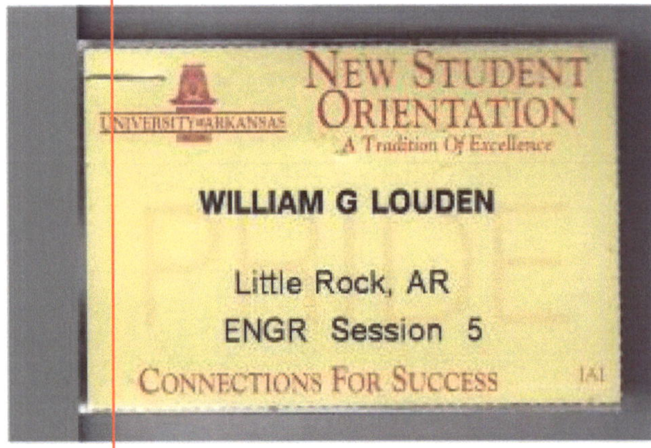

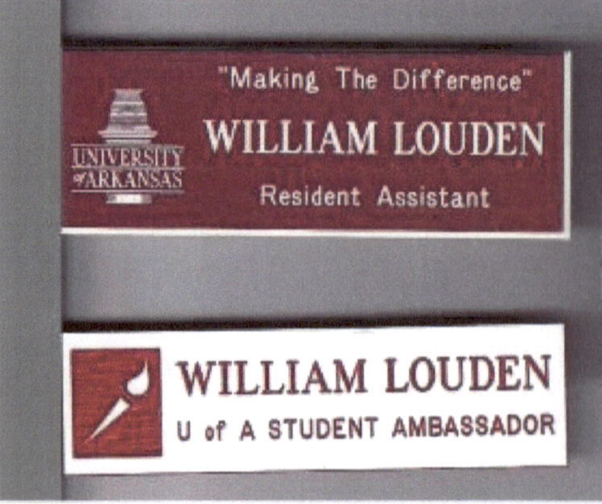

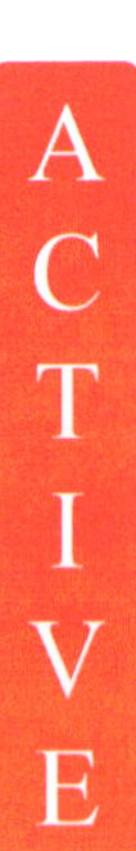

NORTHWEST ARKANSAS TIMES

P.O. Box 1607 • Fayetteville, Arkansas 72702-1607 • (501) 442-1700 • (800) 498-1991 • Fax (501) 442-5477

Michael Whiteley
Times Senior Reporter

January 12, 1999

Virtual Graphx Inc.
Will G. Louden
P. O. Box 2226
Fayetteville, Arkansas 72702-2226

The *Northwest Arkansas Times* Business Section wants to track the development of the region's advertising/public relations industry and to explore its relationship with what has become the fifth fastest growing metropolitan area in the nation.

Our business reporters would like to interview key players in all of the local agencies. But, first, we're asking your agency to answer a few questions that may help us spot trends and frame contexts for the forthcoming interviews.

We ask that you complete this questionnaire and return it to Rusty Garrett, *Times* Business Editor, at the Northwest Arkansas Times, P. O. Box 1607, Fayetteville, 72702, within a week. Please don't hesitate to call me at 442-1750 ext. 139, with any questions.

Your cooperation will assist us in highlighting an important and changing sector of the Northwest Arkansas economy.

Sincerely,

Michael Whiteley

Back in 1999, we received an initial invitation, from an area reporter, to participate in what became our first semi-major regional newspaper write-up. Back then, the *Northwest Arkansas Times*, was one of two daily newspapers, in the region.

This write-up, was a sort of, "game changer," for us, for sure. After that, several other regional write-ups came about. We were on fire.

Sometimes, it's the initial break (or spark), that opens the door for many more future building block breaks to come about!

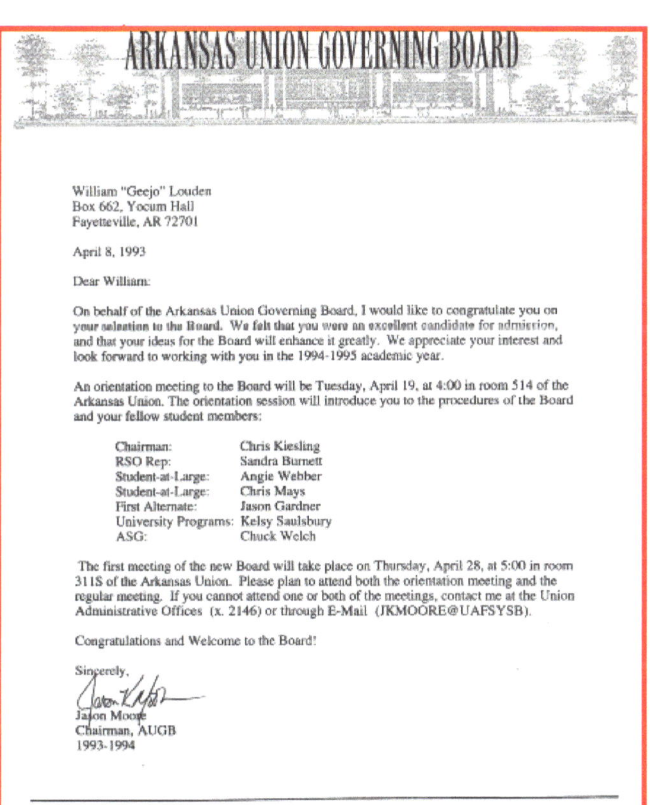

ARKANSAS UNION GOVERNING BOARD

William "Geejo" Louden
Box 662, Yocum Hall
Fayetteville, AR 72701

April 8, 1993

Dear William:

On behalf of the Arkansas Union Governing Board, I would like to congratulate you on your selection to the Board. We felt that you were an excellent candidate for admission, and that your ideas for the Board will enhance it greatly. We appreciate your interest and look forward to working with you in the 1994-1995 academic year.

An orientation meeting to the Board will be Tuesday, April 19, at 4:00 in room 514 of the Arkansas Union. The orientation session will introduce you to the procedures of the Board and your fellow student members:

Chairman:	Chris Kiesling
RSO Rep:	Sandra Burnett
Student-at-Large:	Angie Webber
Student-at-Large:	Chris Mays
First Alternate:	Jason Gardner
University Programs:	Kelsy Saulsbury
ASG:	Chuck Welch

The first meeting of the new Board will take place on Thursday, April 28, at 5:00 in room 311S of the Arkansas Union. Please plan to attend both the orientation meeting and the regular meeting. If you cannot attend one or both of the meetings, contact me at the Union Administrative Offices (x. 2146) or through E-Mail (JKMOORE@UAFSYSB).

Congratulations and Welcome to the Board!

Sincerely,

Jason Moore
Chairman, AUGB
1993-1994

Arkansas Union, Room M423, Fayetteville, Arkansas 72701
(501) 575-2146

President William J. Clinton
and
The William J. Clinton Presidential Foundation
invite you to attend the Topping Out Ceremony
at
The William J. Clinton Presidential Center Construction Site
1200 President Clinton Avenue
Little Rock, Arkansas

Friday, May 23rd, 2003
Gates open 11am, Ceremony begins 12pm

Barbecue lunch hosted by the Jennings Osborne Family
Immediately following the Ceremony
Casual Dress

Parking available on site:
Drive east on 3rd Street. Immediately past the I-30 overpass, take a left on Collins Street.
Parking area will be on the right.
Invitation admits two and is non-transferable. Please present at gate for admission.

Post Office Box 1104
Little Rock, Arkansas 72203-1104

Will G. Louden
P.O. Box 2226
Fayetteville, AR 72702

Chapter 2 ('06 to '07)

Origin Milestones

(5) 2006 One on One, H. Lee Scott,
Wal*Mart, CEO, Magazine Interview;
Northwest Arkansas Living™ Magazine

(6) 2006 NW Arkansas Living
Television™ (Sponsor: Pizza Hut)

(7) 2007 willlouden.com™ Acquired

Ch 2 – 2006 One on One Magazine Interview with H. Lee Scott, Jr., Wal*Mart, CEO

APARTMENTS

Pictures, amenities, deposit, utilities, rental rate information and more can be found online at **nwaliving.com™**

Interacting with a Giant

My Experience Interviewing:

H. Lee Scott, Jr.,

CEO, Wal-Mart Stores, Inc.

By: **Will G. Louden**, Publisher:
Northwest Arkansas Living™ Apartments

Will G. Louden, left and H. Lee Scott, Jr. on right

ROGERS:
Area Code (479)
Breckenridge Apts • 636-3900
2 bedroom, $460 - $495

SPRINGDALE cont:
Eastwood Apts • 927-0676
1 & 2 Bedroom, $415 - $515
Electric Ave Apts • 750-7117

Thursday, March 16, 2006 – It's 5 a.m. and I am wide awake, it's the day of my big break. It's a special day unlike any other

In 2006, after years of high profile interviews, articles and publishing's, etc., arrived an opportunity to sit down with and interview, arguably the largest CEO on Earth?! – Certainly, by employee size?! Wal*Mart, at that time, had the largest private workforce with over 1.5 million employees worldwide!!

APARTMENTS

Pictures, amenities, deposit, utilities, rental rate information and more can be found online at **nwaliving.com™**

A Critical Path to Greatness;

How H. Lee Scott, Jr.,

Climbed to the Top of Wal*Mart

By: **Will G. Louden**, Publisher:
Northwest Arkansas Living™ Apartments

As time passes, some win, and more importantly, some lose. The sun rises and falls, as babies are born and others pass on. The seasons change as disaster remains a sporadic constant component in the life equation. This article, however, is but a spoke in the wheel of life and man's phenomenal successes and triumphs.

ROGERS:
Area Code (479)
Breckenridge Apts • 636-3900
2 bedroom, $460 - $495

SPRINGDALE cont:
Eastwood Apts • 927-0676
1 & 2 Bedroom, $415 - $515
Electric Ave Apts • 750-7117

EDUCATION BEAT

Salute to U of A Walton College Dean, Doyle Z. Williams; The Dawn of a New Era, Dean Williams: This is Your Life

By: **Will G. Louden,**
Publisher: Northwest Arkansas Living™ & Graduating Senior, Walton College of Business

There is something to be said about the triangle of knowledge, the progression and development of society, and the advancement of man. This piece highlights: The road to deanship and what makes the man, and the challenges, accomplishments and prominence of the man for Doyle Zane Williams, Ph.D., retiring Dean of the flagship business school for the state of Arkansas.

Little did the world know that on Dec.18, 1939, in a small town in Louisiana (Natchitoches Parish), a visionary and great leader would be born. The knowledge, perseverance and spirit of a unique and unwavering leader had descended upon this great planet. The husband and father of two, son Zane (B.A. Economics, Rice University; M.S. and Ph.D. Finance, University of California, Berkley), and daughter Elizabeth (A.A. Northwest Arkansas Community College), says that, " The support of my wife, Maynette Derr Williams (B.S. and M.S. Texas Tech University; Ph.D., Ohio State University), has been critical to any success I have enjoyed in my professional career."

Doyle Z. Williams

The Road To Deanship and What Makes The Man

In an article, entitled "Fire, flood, '49 Ford shaped Williams' life," by Bill Bowden, published Feb. 4, 2002, in the Northwest Arkansas Business Journal, Dean Williams describes in vivid detail the early conditions of his childhood and what some would consider an extreme exercise in adversity. Dean Williams tells how the family home burned to the ground Christmas night in 1943, and having to move into "an abandoned sharecropper's house on the bayou." The article also notes how Dean Williams was able to pick his weight in cotton in the 9th grade, "Ninety-nine pounds of cotton in a single day." He also recounts his first experience with a shower after entering Northwestern State University in 1957. This is not exactly the life one would expect such a seasoned and accomplished leader to ascend from, albeit humble beginnings nonetheless.

The seeds of change are in motion by and through the vision, mission and drive of what I will call the "Dean Factor." According to an article entitled "The Quiet Storm," by Alex Daniels of the Arkansas Democrat Gazette, published Oct. 20, 2002, Dean Williams is the human fuel that the academic engine of change burns throughout the Sam M. Walton College of Business at the University of Arkansas at Fayetteville. The "Dean Factor" accelerates the agenda for the next generation of business graduates. In the article, Dr. Karen Pincus, Walton College of Business Accounting Department Chairperson, articulates how the Dean was quick to adapt the accounting curriculum in 1995 to new state CPA examination standards. She said, "In an academic environment, that's unusual." Well, unusual he is as well as very effective!

While Dean Williams believes that "collegiality and willingness to embrace change and not stand on tradition" is a

2[illegible] NORTHWEST ARKANSAS LIVING GUIDE™

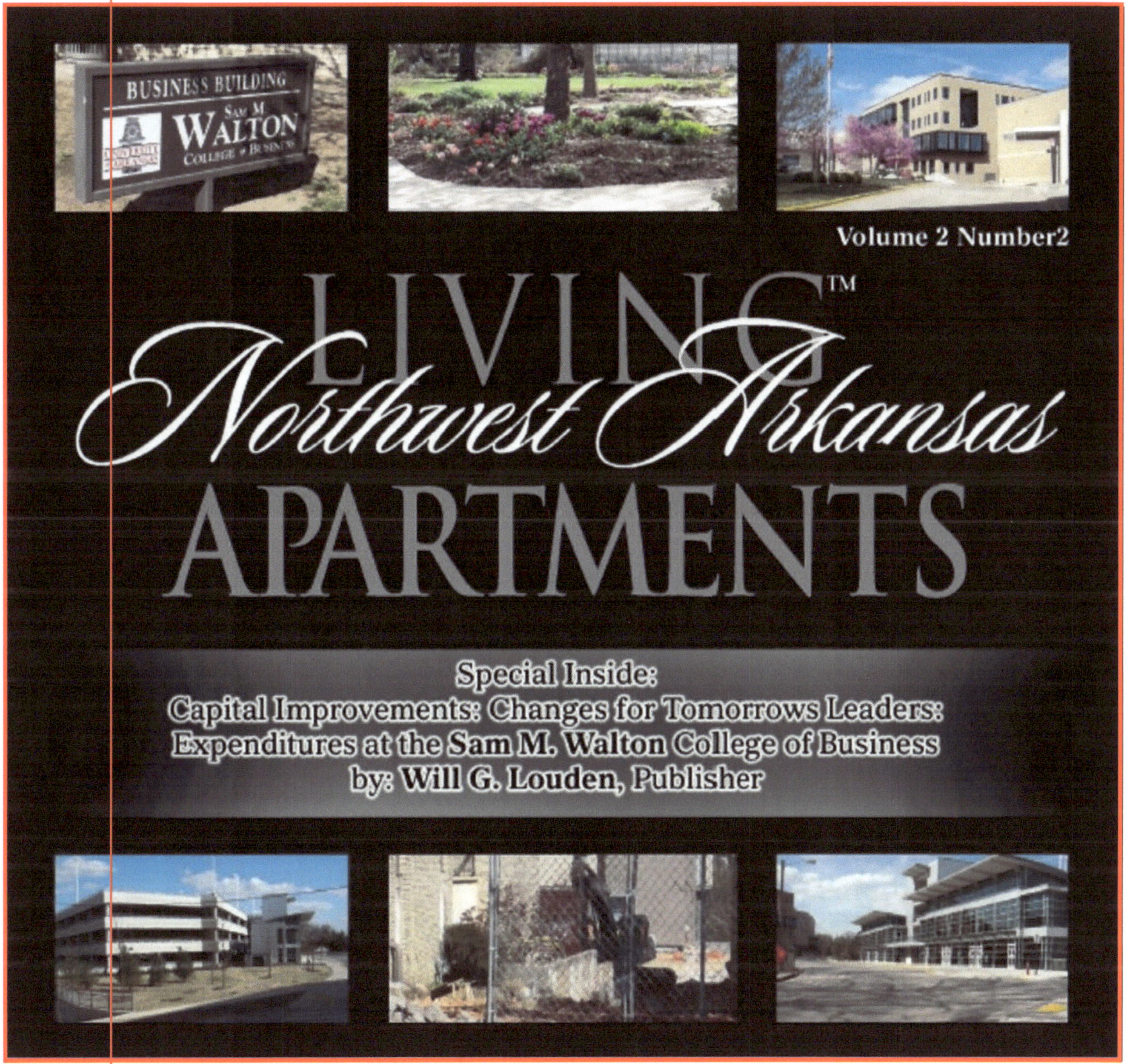

BUSINESS BUILDING
SAM M
WALTON
COLLEGE of BUSINESS

Volume 2 Number2

LIVING™
Northwest Arkansas
APARTMENTS

Special Inside:
Capital Improvements: Changes for Tomorrows Leaders:
Expenditures at the Sam M. Walton College of Business
by: Will G. Louden, Publisher

Today, we publish, "How To," "Corporate Policy," and a number of other genre books under the 13thSquare.com™ literary imprint; those milestones would not have been as possible absent these earlier on magazine publishing credentials.

Cutting our teeth early on, with magazine and Internet publishing's and distribution, really helped to set the stage for many other multimedia, operational and developmental accomplishments down the road.

APARTMENTS

Pictures, amenities, deposit, utilities, rental rate information, addresses, and more can be found online @ nwaliving.com

FAYETTEVILLE cont.:
(Area code 479)
ID #
1038 **White Oaks Apts** • 442-4594
1, 2 & 3 Bedroom, $354 - $660
1139 **Willow Creek Apts** • 442-4594

SPRINGDALE:
(Area code 479)
ID #
1115 **Arbors Apts** • 751-6260
1 & 2 bedroom, $330 - $425
1116 **Black Oak Apts & Twnhms**

***Northwest Arkansas Living Guide*™**
Regular Lifestyle Edition

Revised Production Schedule
Spring 2005: Vol 6, Num 1

Corresponding Tasks:	Important Dates:
Absolute sales & content cutoff	Friday, March 18th, 2005
Publication proof number 1 to Will	Friday, March 25th, 2005
Wills edits back to Mullikin Agency	Monday, March 28th, 2005
Mullikin Agency changes to Will	Wednesday, March 30th, 2005
Will receives final publication proof	Friday, April 01st, 2005
Will's final edits back to Mullikin Agency	Monday, April 04th, 2005
Mullikin Agency sends publication to press	**Wednesday, April 06th, 2005**
Publication back from printer	Wednesday, April 13th, 2005
Publication delivered to Van Buren for insertion	Friday, April 15th, 2005
6,000 Copes released all over the U of A	**Wednesday, April 20th, 2005**
9,000 Copies released all over NWA	Thuesday, April 21st, 2005

Above sample / actual former magazine production schedule.

**Capital Improvements:
Changes for Tomorrows Leaders:
Expenditures at the
Sam M. Walton College of Business**

Commentary By: **Will G. Louden**™ *Publisher: Northwest Arkansas Living*™ & **nwaliving.com**™

He is arguably, without question, one of the greatest business leaders to ever live. With the help of countless individuals, families, firms, and governments, Sam M. Walton created a multi-billion dollar (potentially multi-trillion dollar)empire with all of the trappings of super-

TV Ones' G. Garvin 'Turns up The Heat' at Tyson; "Super Simple" Culinary at Tysons' Discovery Center

By: **Will G. Louden™**
Publisher: Northwest Arkansas Living™ & **nwaliving.com™**

Television superstar and now cookbook author, G. Garvin jammed on into the corporate world headquarters of Tyson Foods (NYSE: TSN) on Wednesday,

Honor & Grace: Saluting Arkansas Icons; *The 2007 Arkansas Business Hall of Fame*

By: **Will G. Louden™**
Publisher: Northwest Arkansas Living™ & ***nwaliving.com™***

U of A Chancellor John White and Wife Mary Lib White

Dr. Maya Angelou Connects with Alltel; Hosts Reception, Spreads Wisdom & Funds Future

By: Will G. Louden,
Publisher:
Northwest Arkansas Living™ Apartments

Arkansas Governor Mike Beebe; Moral Imperative: Excellence

By: ***Will G. Louden™*** (**willglouden.com™**),
Publisher: Northwest Arkansas Living™ & ***nwaliving.com™***
Northwest Arkansas Living ***NEWS™*** Bureau Chief

White marble floors and venerable oak-wood walls encapsulate the conference space off of the main offices for our Arkansas Governor Mike Beebe. He is one of fifty nationwide, a man who wields vast amounts of power and influence. He is a man who appeared to me to be in total control and yes, well healed. And now, the people of the great state of Arkansas have a great leader at the helm.

These various articles and publishing's, from our previous origins, were more than mere milestones; they were, in essence, opportunities to learn, grow, witness, and report on, and to, much larger audiences. Some of these things made us, 'LEGENDARY,' while others made us, 'incredibly grateful!!'

Ch 2 – 2006 Northwest Arkansas Living Television™

Northwest Arkansas Living
5/12/07
Saturday 12:30-1p

Accepted: [signature]
Will G. Louden
Northwest Arkansas Living

[signature]
Laurie R
KARK, KNWA, KFTA
4/18/07

1401 W. Capitol, Suite 104 Little Rock, Arkansas 72201
501.340.4444 501.376.2957 (fax) www.arkansasmatters.com

Another propelling origin milestone, that deserves a mention, was the time we inked our first ever statewide (practically), full power, broadcast television show deal.

To the left is the redacted agreement, the terms of which could be considered graciously, lucrative!!

The airtime was purchased at a truly exceptional rate causing keen brand expansion, once again across multimedia platforms!!

Here, VGIS produced the show(s), and/or collaborated / partnered to have them produced, at an extreme high quality, before finally editing them and sending them to the mother station in the chain to be broadcast, statewide!!

We actually also received a nice sponsorship from Pizza Hut, who helped to shoulder the cost of our, ***10-year anniversary show***. They also let us use one of their restaurants to tape the show.

Print your boarding pass at continental.com 24 hours before your flight

Issue Date June 03, 2007

eTicket Itinerary and Receipt

eTicket Confirmation: **CQ2EVM**

Day	Date	Flight/ Class	Depart	Time	Arrive	Time	Equip	Meal
Tue	26JUN07	CO 2297 L	Northwest Arkansas	6:25 PM	Houston-Bush Intl	8:05 PM	ERJ 145	
		Operated by ExpressJet Airlines doing business as Continental Express						
Tue	26JUN07	CO 595 L	Houston-Bush Intl	10:55 PM	Los Angeles	12:20 AM	737-800	
Tue	17JUL07	CO 794 L	Los Angeles	5:35 AM	Houston-Bush Intl	10:51 AM	737-800	Snack
Tue	17JUL07	CO 2413 L	Houston-Bush Intl	12:25 PM	Northwest Arkansas	1:52 PM	ERJ-135	
		Operated by ExpressJet Airlines doing business as Continental Express						

Traveler (1)	Frequent Flyer	eTicket Number	Seat(s)
LOUDEN / WILL		0057051442819	10A/5E/9D/6A

Fare: $174.88 **Combined Tax:** $45.72 **Per Person Total:** $220.60 **eTicket Total:** $220.60

Method of Payment: Visa XXXXXXXXXXXX2205

Continental Airlines

Name: LOUDEN/WILL
Date: TUE 26 JUN 2007 29

CQ2EVM
Flight: CO 2297 L Operated by ExpressJet Airlines

Gate: **B4** Seat: **10A**

Depart: Northwest Arkansas 6:25 PM
Arrive: Houston-Bush Intl 8:05 PM
Board Time: 5:50 PM

eTicket 00570514428190 **eTicket** Boarding Pass

Continental Airlines

Name: LOUDEN/WILL
Date: TUE 26 JUN 2007 30

CQ2EVM
Flight: CO 595 L

Gate: **E2** *Gate May Change; Check Before Departure* Seat: **5E**

Depart: Houston-Bush Intl 10:55 PM
Arrive: Los Angeles 12:20 AM
Board Time: 10:20 PM

eTicket 00570514428190 **eTicket** Boarding Pass

In 2007, we flew across country to meet, engage and tape an interview with arguably one of the largest full broadcast television and media executives ever. Back then, Mr. Ed Wilson, was THE President of THE FOX Television Network, which at that time was the producer / broadcaster / distributor, etc. etc., of the super smash hit reality television show, "***American Idol***."

When we received the opportunity to go, we didn't hesitate, we packed up, moved Heaven and Earth, and did whatever was required, to not only make the trip happen, but to also make sure that it was a rousing success as well!!

Ch 2 – 2007 willlouden.com™ is Acquired

CERTIFICATE

of Domain Ownership

Awarded to:

Will Louden

for the successful renewal of:

willlouden.com

renewed on 03 Mar. 2025 | valid through 26 Apr. 2026

This certificate is issued by:
ResellersPanel.com / LiquidNet Ltd.

The WHOIS information of this domain is publicly available

Several years would pass along with an initial volunteer teaching trip out to Eastern Europe, before the ***willlouden.com***™ domain name, would become: willlouden.com, Inc., in 2012, a Wyoming chartered C-Corporation.

This strategic decision and origin milestone to acquire the willlouden.com™ BRAND, post the VGIS era, occurred, in earnest, after returning from an otherwise whirlwind stint, out to LA meeting and engaging one of the biggest, influential, and most powerful, television and multimedia executives on the planet. This move set forth a solid foundation for our current ecosystem, to launch and position for even higher levels than all previous predecessors…

Chapter 3 (2008)

Origin Milestones

(8) 2008 Hollywood Playboy Mansion (Sponsor: Dillard's) | Cops and Robbers Charity Event | Dillard's Male Model

Ch 3 – 2008 Hollywood Playboy Mansion Cops and Robbers Charity Function

Partying and networking at THE Hollywood Playboy Mansion was clearly a colossal experience indeed, but it was also, without any doubt, a monumental career achievement milestone as well; no matter what your orientation, social status, and/or ever ending persuasion, etc. etc., the atmosphere of a bona fide Hollywood sequence of events is not to be underestimated and/or taken lightly. We were invited, we attended, and we appreciated the opportunity!!

PUDER
PRODUCTIONS

XL prints

To this day, we don't really know how we were placed on the Hollywood Playboy Mansion, invitee list; we have some ideas, but no absolute definitive knowledge.

When we received the invitation we immediately approached, Arkansas based Dillard's, to possibly assist with sponsorship, to which they happily obliged, and as true neighbors, and friends in business, we invited one of their store associates to tag along as an assistant and plus one. It was epic.

Mr. David Gerdel (dxxxxxel@aol.com),
General Manager, Dillard's
Northwest Arkansas Mall
Fayetteville, Arkansas 72703

Dear Mr. Gerdel:

Thank you for accepting my phone call yesterday and talking with me about the once in a lifetime invitation I received two weeks ago to attend a VIP Hollywood Red Carpet event partially benefiting the exceptionally worthwhile and worthy *Cops Care Cancer Foundation*. The *Cops Care Cancer Foundation* supports the Lucile Packard Children's Hospital and children (and their families) who have been stricken with cancer.

For your interest and further review I have included along with this letter two DVD's that contain three previously produced television shows. One is our premier television show featuring Wal*Mart Stores, Inc. (which broadcast in December 2006 regionally on KNWA-TV (NBC)). That DVD also contains a 30-minute interview of me which broadcast back in November/2006 on KNWA as well. The other DVD contains an exclusive interview with our Governor, Mike Beebe which broadcast back in May of 2007, statewide on KARK-TV...

(NBC), KNWA-TV (NBC) as well as KFTA-TV (FOX). I have also enclosed several copies of our past previous magazines for your interest and review as well. I have also included an event flier, as well as several media/press releases about me, my company and some of the things we are involved in. Also attached is a most recent abbreviated career vita of me for your review as well.

The remaining, unedited, aspects of this sponsorship request letter as well as the resulting terms of the eventual deal / sponsorship is hereby omitted…

For more information please visit: ***13thSquare.com***™

Pictured above is the Santa Monica Pier, which we toured while we were out partying and networking at THE Hollywood Playboy Mansion.

Also, to arrive at THE Hollywood Playboy Mansion, we first had to arrive at a secure designated area located on the UCLA campus. There, we were escorted directly to and through those hollowed gates of, THE Hollywood Playboy Mansion (SIDE NOTE: When we arrived, my invited Dillard's employee guest, wasn't on the guest list, and was initially not allowed in. After I raised a light fuss (lol), saying that if he wasn't allowed in, then I, too, wasn't going in… A few moments later, security returned and allowed us BOTH in… Magnificent)!!

Thank you Dillard's!!

Chapter 4 ('11 to '12)

Origin Milestones

(9) 2011 Ceased Operating VGIS, Inc.

(10) 2011 Georgia / Eastern Europe
Invitee (Sept. to Dec.) K-12 English as a
Second Language Volunteer Teacher

(11) 2012 willlouden.com, Inc.
Chartered / Formed (in February)

Again, here is a volunteer English teaching opportunity that was much more than just a simple major life milestone, for us. This is the sort of life changing experience that not only impacts the communities where we engaged, but it also changed and impacted our lives as well as the lives of other volunteers.

The apparent selection process for becoming an actual volunteer was somewhat challenging, yet also extremely rewarding, as well. The process of fulfilling the mission was nearly equally as grueling once selected as preparing to travel over and make it through the full week of intense training and orientation. Working with the children, staying with a host family and engaging, fully, in the culture, were all experiences that enhanced our origin story in ways that enhance our vast developing journey even to this day.

After flying all day, and what seemed like all night too, we eventually arrived at our destination county. Upon landing, we were checked into the country and then whisked away to the host hotel which was really akin to an apparent, “host palace!”

After an initial night of hello's and welcomes, etc., we awoke the next morning to a trip to the medical office to get blood tests, and then a full week of orientation and training before eventually departing the capital city for parts truly unknown with our respective host families. The goal was to teach (English as a second language) after the orientation.

Class Schedule

My Weekly Grade School (Class) Schedule
16 to 19 Total Instructional Hours/Week Average
Will G. Louden™ (willglouden.com™)

Monday:

Class/Break	**Period**	**Co-Teacher**	**Length**	**Grade Level**
1) Class	9:00 a.m. – 9:45 a.m.	Inga	45 Minutes	1st Grade
2) Class	9:55 a.m. – 10:40 a.m.	Inga	45 Minutes	4th Grade
3) Class	10:50 a.m. – 11:35 a.m.	Tsira	45 Minutes	6th Grade

Tuesday:

Class/Break	**Period**	**Co-Teacher**	**Length**	**Grade Level**
1) Class	9:00 a.m. – 9:45 a.m.	Tsira	45 Minutes	5th Grade
2) Class	9:55 a.m. – 10:40 a.m.	Inga	45 Minutes	1st Grade
*- BREAK	10:50 a.m. – 11:35 a.m.	BREAK	1 hour	BREAK
3) Class	11:55 a.m. – 12:40 p.m.	Inga	45 Minutes	2nd Grade

Wednesday:

Class/Break	**Period**	**Co-Teacher**	**Length**	**Grade Level**
1) Class	9:00 a.m. – 9:45 a.m.	Tsira	45 Minutes	5th Grade
2) Class	9:55 a.m. – 10:40 a.m.	Tsira	45 Minutes	6th Grade
3) Class	10:50 a.m. – 11:35 a.m.	Inga	45 Minutes	4th Grade
*- BREAK	11:55 a.m. – 12:35 p.m.	BREAK	1 hour	BREAK
4) Class	12:50 p.m. – 13:35 p.m.	Inga	45 Minutes	3rd Grade

Thursday:

Class/Break	**Period**	**Co-Teacher**	**Length**	**Grade Level**
1) Class	9:00 a.m. – 9:45 a.m.	Inga	45 Minutes	4th Grade
*- BREAK	10:00 a.m. – 10:35 a.m.	BREAK	45 Minutes	BREAK
2) Class	10:50 a.m. – 11:35 a.m.	Inga	45 Minutes	1st Grade
*- BREAK	11:50 a.m. – 12:35 p.m.	BREAK	1 Hour	BREAK
3) Class	12:50 p.m. – 13:35 p.m.	Inga	45 Minutes	2nd Grade

Friday:

Class/Break	**Period**	**Co-Teacher**	**Length**	**Grade Level**
1) Class	9:00 a.m. – 9:45 a.m.	Inga	45 Minutes	3rd Grade
2) Class	10:00 a.m. – 10:35	Tsira	45 Minutes	5th Grade
2) Class	10:50 a.m. – 11:35	Tsira	45 Minutes	6th Grade

Geocell
MARKET

A day visit to the, "end laws," one weekend, produced food, drink and a quick tour of the property / tool shed. It was all completely an, "experience!!"

In addition to teaching K-12 classes, everyday, we were also responsible for teaching host family children as well. . . Some of the other volunteers from the international program even taught some adults too, on the side, for extra income.

THE ***Black Sea*** is beautiful and where it all went down. These were all experiences which were leveraged to last longer than a lifetime!!

One former key milestone which may have contributed heavily towards our selection into this particular international program was likely that of our previous past of being magazine and multimedia broadcasters and publishers, etc.

SECURITY
043 C

Chapter 5 (2012)

Origin Milestones

(12) 2012 Obama Reelection Campaign
(Volunteer) | "*Obama Fellow*"

Max Maxfield, WY Secretary of State
FILED: 02/16/2012 03:01 PM
ID: 2012-000616928

ARTICLES OF INCORPORATION OF

WILLLOUDEN.COM, INC.

A Wyoming Corporation

<u>ARTICLE I</u>
NAME

The name of the Corporation is **WILLLOUDEN.COM**.

This Corporation Name is used under perpetual License granted from the firm founder, William Gorden Louden ("Licensor") to WILL LOUDEN, LLC ("Licensee"), a state of Arkansas Limited Liability Company, and "WILLLOUDEN.COM, Inc." ("Sub-Licensee"), in a general "Trademark/Brand and License Agreement," executed in 2012.

The terms and conditions of usage, (the "License") may be obtained from the Secretary of the Corporation upon request.

<u>ARTICLE II</u>
REGISTERED OFFICE AND AGENT

The address of the Corporation's registered office in the State of Wyoming is:

InCorp Services, Inc.
1621 Central Ave.
Cheyenne, WY 82001

02/07/12

The name of its registered agent at such address is: <u>Josie A. Sorensen</u>.

WILLLOUDEN.COM, Inc. (Wyoming) Articles of Incorporation 1

In Feb. 2012, willlouden.com, Inc. began under the laws of Wyoming, USA.

In 2012, after returning from a truly amazing volunteer ESL teacher experience in Eastern Europe, we received an, *invitation to apply*, to join THE Obama reelection campaign… We applied. We made Florida our ONLY choice. We were accepted – and the rest is HISTORY!! :_) lol

Subject: We're looking for Obama organizing fellows

From: Sara El-Amine, BarackObama.com (info@barackobama.com)

To: ;

Date: Monday, December 5, 2011 6:35 AM

2012 BARACKOBAMA.COM

Will --

Know anyone who wants to go above and beyond to help re-elect President Obama in 2012?

Obama for America and Organizing for America are looking for bright, motivated people for our Organizing Fellowship Program -- a 12-week program that will be held three times in 2012: during the spring, the summer, and the fall.

Here's why you should think about it… (the remainder of this email invitation has been omitted from this book).

Subject: Will G. Louden – Obama Fellowship Acceptance. 05.29.12.

Charlotte:

Pursuant to your interview/conversation on last Friday I've spoken to several members of my family and subsequently made arrangements to have a car as required to complete the appointment!

I have also communicated my commitment and potential role as an "Obama Fellow" to all boards, committees, and organizations, etc. where I play a role. I have and continue to make arrangements to be out of the area for as long as Needed to honor this new commitment!

I am also working on delaying my South African trip until after the election IF necessary.

Acceptance as an "*Obama Organizing Fellow*!!"

Subject: Acceptance to Summer Organizer Program
From: Charlotte Nugent

Date: Monday, June 4, 2012 11:56 AM

Dear Will,

Congratulations! You were selected out of thousands of applicants for the Obama Organizing Fellowship in Florida! You were chosen because of your commitment to this President and the unique organizer potential we saw in you through our interview process. Please reply right away to confirm your acceptance of our offer to join the program.

You are a part of the largest presidential campaign organizing fellowship in United States history and the work you do here will have real impact—the summer of 2012 is a critical time for our country. You will be part of a national effort that registers, persuades, and turns out millions of voters to help prepare us for November 6, 2012. A lot is at stake, and Election Day is nearing. We can't wait for you to get organizing!

Please mark your calendar for two important dates: June 16 and June 19. In order to prepare you for success in your role as a Summer Organizing Fellow, you'll be attending a full day kickoff training near you on Saturday, June 16. After the kickoff training, you'll get started organizing in your region with an orientation on Tuesday, June 19. These two trainings are critical to your success, and are only the beginning—we'll provide ongoing training and support throughout the summer. We will provide additional details on these trainings in the coming weeks.

Please let me know if you have any questions. We look forward to working with you!

Inside an ***Obama*** campaign office, there's a lot of extremely high energy and constant activity!! These weren't boring places. Meetings, phone banks, speeches, etc. all filled the space constantly. The energy is practically always high. The only times when the energy may not have been high would be at the open and/or close of a day and perhaps when there's an outside of the office event where a lot of staff and volunteers may be out working the event and/or canvassing a neighborhood, etc.

Working and volunteering at an official Obama reelection event, in a very BIG state, like Florida, isn't a small feat, to say the least. All of the elements of a major live event are present, including: crowd control, lighting, sound and security, etc. – it is completely an experience and another keen part of our origin journey!!

← Back

Obama National Oct 2012

Required Action for Your Volunteer Role with the Presidential Inaugural Committee

Allison Panther
apanther@2013pic.org

Thank you so much for your commitment to volunteering with the Inaugural Balls Team! As a part of your official volunteer function with the Inaugural Balls at the 57th Presidential Inaugural Ceremonies, you are required to register for a United States Secret Service (USSS) issued credential. In addition to submitting your personal information, the application also requires a photo submission, guidelines are below.

In order to access the application, use the following link and password:
https://donate.2013pic.org/page/content/staff-volunteers-vendors-registration
Password: Obama*Biden*2013!

Notes about application:

- Employer is PIC
- Function is pic_volunteer
- I have a working role at Inaugural Ball/Commander-in-Chief (please only check this box)

Another very astonishing feat, if not an incredibly awesome milestone, was in not only being selected as a key, "*floater member*," of the *Presidential Inaugural Balls Team*, but in also being invited and subsequently granted, **PIC** (***Presidential Inaugural Committee***), and USSS (***United States Secret Service***) credentials. That whole entire process was completely a learning experience!

After he won though, and before these particular milestones were achieved, we were also invited to THE, "*Arkansas Governor's Christmas Party*," at THE *Arkansas Governors Mansion*, which were surreal experiences, to be sure.

When we first received the, "invitation to apply," to join the president's reelection campaign, little did we know and/or have absolutely any idea, just how fruitfully fulfilling, soul rejuvenating, and/or knowledgeably rewarding, the whole entire experience would be.

This milestone literally allowed for and made way to a near limitless kindred human interaction sequence, as well as a truly whirlwind everywhere and anywhere complete travel experience, too.

Although, some of us were mere staff and volunteers, in some ways we, too, were running for President!! Wow. What a Wow!! Incredible Experience!

The first time you drive from Tampa through the Florida Keys to Key West is completely priceless and goes far beyond a mere milestone experience. These experiences are apart of our origin story. They are what refine and define us on this journey!!

Chapter 6 (2013)

Origin Milestones

(13) 2013 20-Yr Class Reunion Volunteer (Sponsor: Coke) | Chairman, Little Rock Parkview Arts/Science Magnet High School Class of '93, 20-Year Class Reunion Organizing Committee, PV93.ORG

Another crucial milestone for us was the time when we led a semi large scale community event where hundreds attended. Coke also signed on as an official beverage sponsor for the events (of the weekend).

Producing a highly successful event, with Coke as a sponsor, felt really good!! The practice of giving back to support communities is a deep seed of our origin DNA!!

Arts/Science Magnet High School

Class of 1993 20-Year Reunion Itinerary July 4th – 7th Little Rock, AR

Friday, July 5th

Reunion Check in/School Tour
Location: Parkview Arts/Science Magnet High School
Address | Time and Description – All Omitted

Informal Mix and Mingle/Meet and Greet
Location: Parkview High School
Address | Time and Description – All Omitted

Saturday, July 6th

Family Picnic in the Park
Location: Parkview High School
Address | Time and Description – All Omitted

Awards Banquet & Comedy Show
Location: Parkview High School
Address | Time and Description – All Omitted

Sunday, July 7th

Prayer Breakfast
Location: Parkview Magnet High School
Address | Time and Description – All Omitted

Morning Church Service
Location: Parkview High School
Address | Time and Description – All Omitted

Special Shout Out & Thanks to our Reunion Venues, Vendors, Sponsors and Friends (Note, most have been omitted from this publication):

Wal*Mart Stores | WILLLOUDEN.COM, Inc. | War Memorial Park | Office Depot | Parkview High School Revolution Food and Music | Coca Cola Also Thank You to the Class of 1993 Members & Guests Present

The class reunion and all of its planned / scheduled events and functions, etc. all came off without any noticeable glitches. From all accounts, everyone in attendance appeared to dance, sing, eat, drink, and fully enjoy themselves as well as others. Reunions, are for re-gathering, reminiscing, and planning for the future. This milestone was truly one for the record and history books!!

Here we achieve yet another critical milestone with the strategic listing of the ***willlouden.com***, Inc. BRAND as one of the top five reunion sponsors and event underwriters.

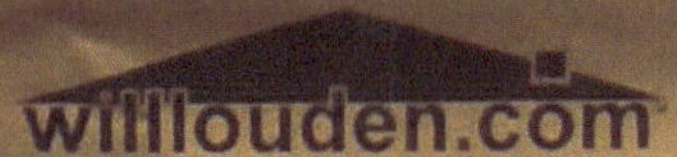

Producing this community centered event, which was actually a twenty-year class reunion, was a 'class effort.' Key members from the class all chipped in – financially, professionally, as well as creatively, to help produce everything from the tee-shirt design, to the professional entertainment, for the banquet. Seeing friends and families all come together and enjoy themselves was also a class act in and of itself.

A plaque for the school, from the class, in honor of a very high achievement!!

PV93.org and the Parkview Class of 1993
hereby recognizes the

PARKVIEW ARTS/SCIENCE MAGNET H.S.
AND LITTLE ROCK SCHOOL DISTRICT

for achieving the

"4TH BEST HIGH SCHOOL"
In the State of Arkansas

and

"249TH BEST HIGH SCHOOL"
In the Nation

Ranking as Recognized by the Washington Post

Congratulations on this stunning achievement!

CLASS OF 1993 - 20 YEAR REUNION
JULY 6, 2013

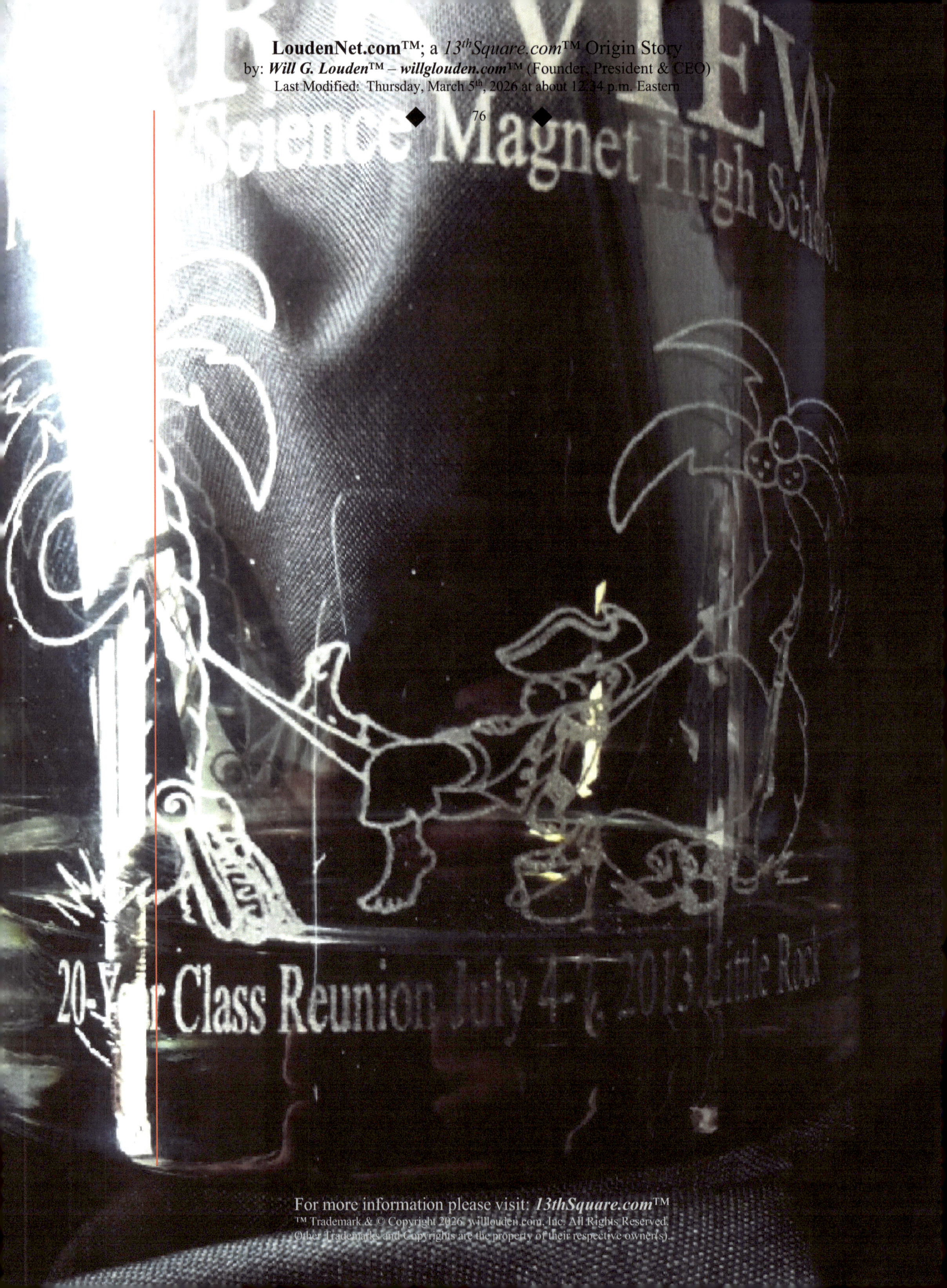
Science Magnet High
Class Reunion July 4-7, 2013 Little Rock

While the most critical aspects of this reunion were bright and shinny, it really was a team effort to achieve this particular milestone. Did we manage our way through challenges, yes; absolutely!! Were those challenges insurmountable, no; absolutely, they were not.

From the custom cake, to the custom engraved classes, to the custom logo, and the custom tees, etc.; the reunion was profitable and one for the record books.

You might even say that this was a milestone that produced many other exceptional milestones and achievable(s), which were all more than worthy to enjoy, celebrate, and ultimately: be proud of!!

One of the things (secrets), that we strategically employed, to help make this particular reunion, extra special, and wildly successful, were the preorder tickets. We knew exactly what everyone wanted to eat at the banquet before the night of the banquet. We provided this information to the banquet / restaurant partner to help control costs and ensure a delightful, and most memorable, (dinner) experience!

We also took preorders for tee-shirts; the shirts were printed in two colors and practically all sizes; we also employed various other mechanisms for helping to determine some of the finer things that members of the class would like to see happen during the reunion. Lastly, after all is said and done, one must ask, if it all met the mark?! I think we exceeded it?!

Arts/Science Magnet High School
Class of 1993 20 Year Class Reunion

Little Rock Parkview

20 Year Class Reunion

PV93.ORG™

Committee/Board Members

Will G. Louden™
Chairman
chairman@pv93.org

PRESS/MEDIA RELEASE

Parkview Class of 1993 Set to Recognize Little Rock School District for Outstanding State/National Ranking in July

For More: pv93.org/pressmedia.htm

To: Associated Press/Arkansas Media (All Media) & all media wires
From/By: PV93.ORG; ***Will G. Louden***™ (willglouden.com™),
Chairman: PV93.ORG, Inc. (chairman@pv93.org)

For Immediate Release.

Release Date: Monday, June 17th, 2013

Parkview Class of 1993 Set to Recognize Little Rock School District for Outstanding State/National Ranking in July

Little Rock, Arkansas – Today, ***Will G. Louden***™ (willglouden.com™), Chairman of PV93.ORG, Inc. (PV93.ORG™), announced plans to recognize the Little Rock School District and the current administration of Parkview Arts/Science Magnet High School for achieving a ranking of 4th in Arkansas and 249th in the nation by the Washington Post.

Arts/Science Magnet High School
Class of 1993 20 Year Class Reunion

Little Rock Parkview

20 Year Class Reunion

PV93.ORG™

Committee/Board Members

Will G. Louden™
Chairman
chairman@pv93.org

PRESS/MEDIA RELEASE

PV93.ORG, Inc. and the Parkview Class of 1993 Completes Successful 20-Year Class Reunion, Recognizes Absent LRSD

For more: pv93.org/pressmedia.htm

To: Associated Press/Arkansas Media (All Media) & all media wires
From/By: PV93.org; ***Will G. Louden***™ (willglouden.com™), Chairman:
PV93.org, Inc. (chairman@pv93.org)

For Immediate Release.

Release Date: Tuesday, July 9th, 2013

PV93.ORG, Inc. and the Parkview Class of 1993 Completes Successful 20-Year Class Reunion, Recognizes Absent LRSD

Little Rock, Arkansas – Today, ***Will G. Louden***™ (willglouden.com™), outgoing Chairman of PV93.org, Inc., "*Chairman Emeritus*," announced the completion of a very successful Parkview class of 1993 20-year class reunion weekend. We pulled in an estimated US $7,500 from registration fees, tee shirt sales, picture and video sales, etc. Another US $5,000 to US $7,000 of 'in kind donations' and/or sponsor/vendor and friend contributions helped to make the reunion weekend extra special!

Chapter 7 ('14 to '16)

Origin Milestones

(14) 2014 Memphis Whole Home Renovation

(15) 2016 WHR Book Series Initial Draft Written (unpublished)

In 2014, we commenced to renovating a small house. That milestone took a little over a full year to accomplish. At the end of the renovation, in 2016, we started writing several, "how to books," from a, beginners, perspective. This is the origins of both the diyNovice.com™ (whole home renovation brand), and the 13thSquare.com™, literary imprint, brand.

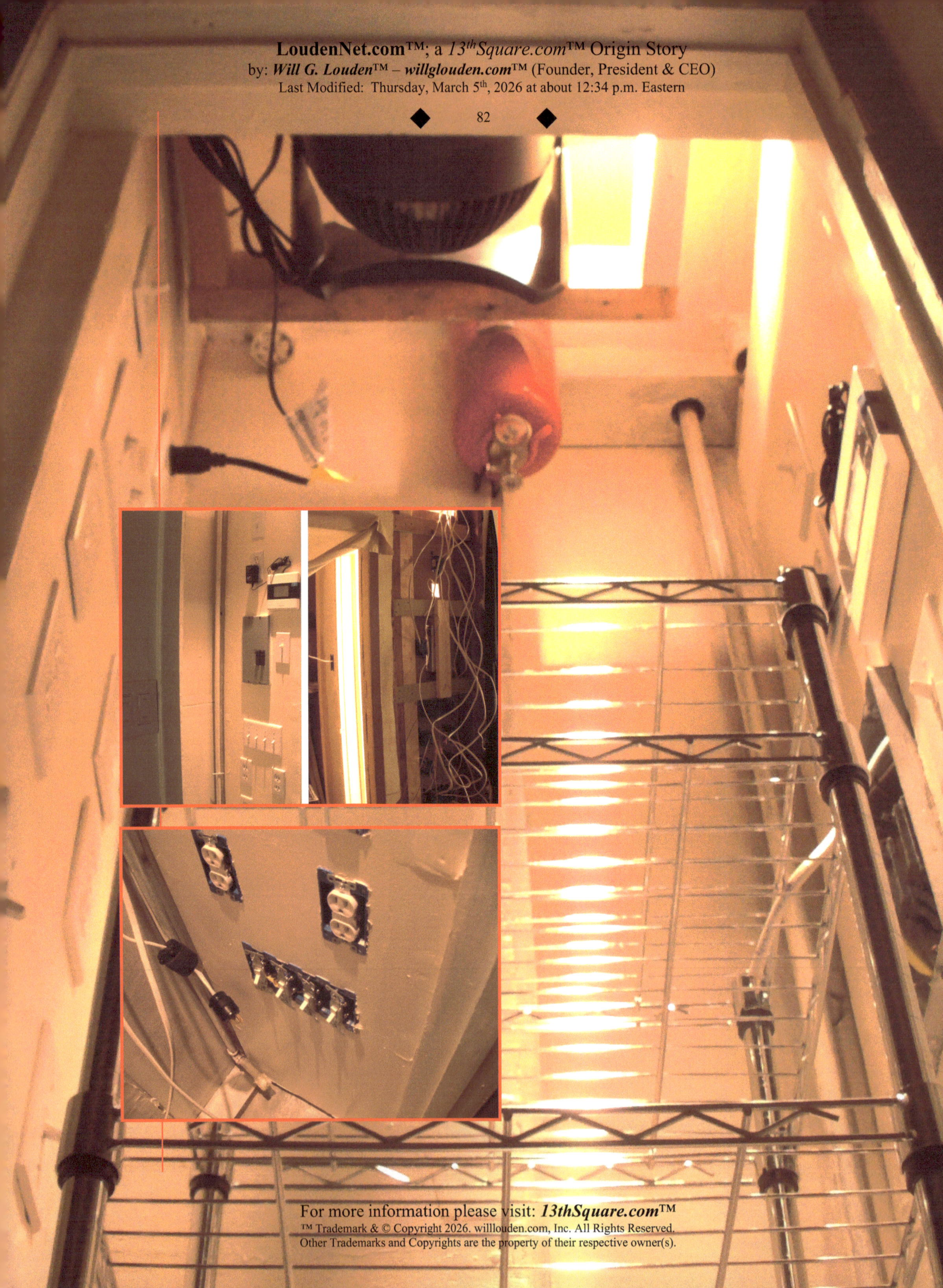

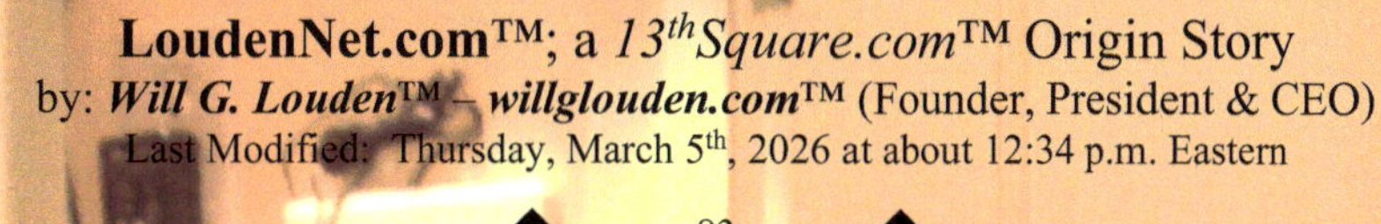

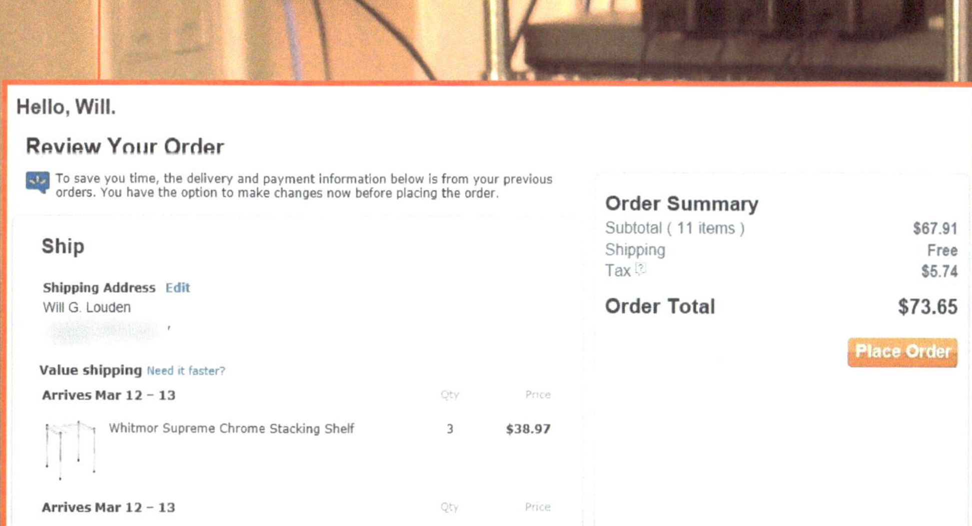
Hello, Will.

Review Your Order

To save you time, the delivery and payment information below is from your previous orders. You have the option to make changes now before placing the order.

Ship

Shipping Address Edit
Will G. Louden

Value shipping Need it faster?

Arrives Mar 12 – 13	Qty	Price
Whitmor Supreme Chrome Stacking Shelf	3	$38.97

Arrives Mar 12 – 13 Qty Price

Order Summary

Subtotal (11 items)	$67.91
Shipping	Free
Tax	$5.74
Order Total	**$73.65**

Place Order

11:40 PM
3/4/2015

This wire shelving played a critical role in the final build out of this smart closet, which was a very strategic part of this, "Whole Home Renovation."

The whole entire process of building a, "Laundry Closet," from scratch, for the first time ever, and alone, as a novice – lol, was completely an experience; however, it too, was yet another critical origin milestone for sure.

Also, during the whole home renovation, we endeavored to convert an old towel and linen closet into a fully tiled, water tight and semi luxury shower. Is this another, "origin milestone?!" We think so!!

And in another extremely awesome first (origin story milestone and potentially last – lol) time we were introduced to this very special tool; It's a special diamond blade: Wet. Tile. Saw.

89

◆ ◆

8.11.16

Hi Will,

I'm so glad we could be so helpful and were able to take care of you!

We're dying to see the finished product so definitely let us know when you have done! :)

Your Apex heater shipped today from Vancouver, WA via Fedex and the tracking number is 702039211829.

We're always here to help so please keep our contact info and let us know if you have any questions.

Thanks Will!

Best regards,
Kerri

8.21.16 diyNovice.com

Greetings Kerri:

I have installed ALL of the heaters (pictures attached) including the Apex72 (LOVE THAT ONE!!) and they are ALL working nicely!!! :_) BIG JOB!!

I'm grateful to #TeamCadet and #TeamDepot for the consideration(s)!!

The house is now complete which means that I can finally refocus my energies onto diy book(s) AND related media development. I anticipate it taking upwards of 3 to 6 months or so to accomplish this task. I will follow up with you/Jon WHEN I'm done (or near done) to talk joint promotion!

Thanks again for everything!!

Sincerely,

Will

Chapter 8 ('20 to '21)

Origin Milestones

(16) 2020 NJIT Capstone (Sponsor: Frank B.; Spring 2020) | Initial Team Multi Year, Multi Team Sponsor / Partner

(17) 2021 Full Emersion into the NJIT on Campus Experience

(18) 2021 GMIS Attendee; Dubai King Invitee (VP UAE) (Nov.)

(19) 2021 First Visit to Africa || Kenya, Africa First Visit

Another origin milestone, that we received all along the way, was an invitation to visit Samsungs Manhattan, New York, USA offices. wow… Grateful!!

2019 Developer 5G Series
presented by
Samsung and Verizon 5G Lab

Congratulations! Your Spring 2020 Capstone Project is approved. What is next?

OE Osama Eljabiri
To: 'Eljabiri,, Cc: 'Charles · Sat, Jan 25, 2020 at 8:51 AM

Dear Capstone Spring 2020 Sponsor,

Congratulations! Your project proposal is approved. If you have submitted more than one proposal of requested multiple teams for your project, this has been approved as well.

You are officially invited to our mandatory Spring 2020 Capstone Projects Open House on

When: Saturday, Feb 1st, 2020 12 PM-5 PM

Where: NJIT's Campus Center Atrium

In addition to becoming official NJIT Capstone sponsors, the whole entire student life experience was too, a bit of a milestone!!

Seven years. Thirty-six teams. And one-hundred-eighty plus student interns later, we're extremely grateful for the NJIT relationship and milestone. It's a very productive relationship / partnership.

From multiple student MVP wins, to several team placements, to even a few top project manager standouts, the origin story is sound and profound throughout the whole entire NJIT student Capstone experience!! Thank you, NJIT!! :_)

Origin milestone; yes, but also, completely an EXPERIENCE.

To be honest, one of the absolute best parts of the initial (and subsequent), NJIT on boarding experience / milestone, etc., was the entire campus life experience, and the food, by far – THE FOOD?!! YES!!

Ch 8 – 2022 Dubai GMIS Attendance by Invitation of THE King

GMIS Global Manufacturing & Industrialisation Summit

Co-Host — DUBAI ECONOMY | Co-Chair & Co-Host | Co-Chair

22-27 NOVEMBER 2021 | DUBAI EXHIBITION CENTRE

Brought to you by

ADNOC MUBADALA

WILL G LOUDEN

CHIEF EXECUTIVE OFFICER

WILLLOUDEN.COM

UNITED STATES

29727111222481

DELEGATE

After a truly horrific global pandemic and a few very successful cycles, with the NJIT Capstone project, the invitation of invitations arrived by way of Dubai from THE King. We proudly attended the GMIS industrialization summit, and upon completion made another milestone, which was visiting Africa for the first time too – Kenya.

Chapter 9 (2022)

Origin Milestones

(20) 2022 Tanzania, Africa Initial Visit

(21) 2022 United Nations Africa/US Trade Event (Nigerian Led) African Union NYC Meeting Room Invitee / Attendee

(22) 2022 PangeaSoul.com™ NJIT Student Team Wins 1st Place in the Midterms (March) || Project Manager Wins MVP

(23) 2022 1st Trip out to Silicon Valley (Sponsor: API: World) (October)

Ch 9 – 2022 1st Ever Time Visiting Zanibar Tanzania, Africa

Landing in Zanzibar, Tanzania, after a really nice trip to Mombasa, Kenya, was in one word a milestone, but in another word – magnificent. We are honored that its apart of our origin!

By the way, the East African beaches are very, very beautiful!

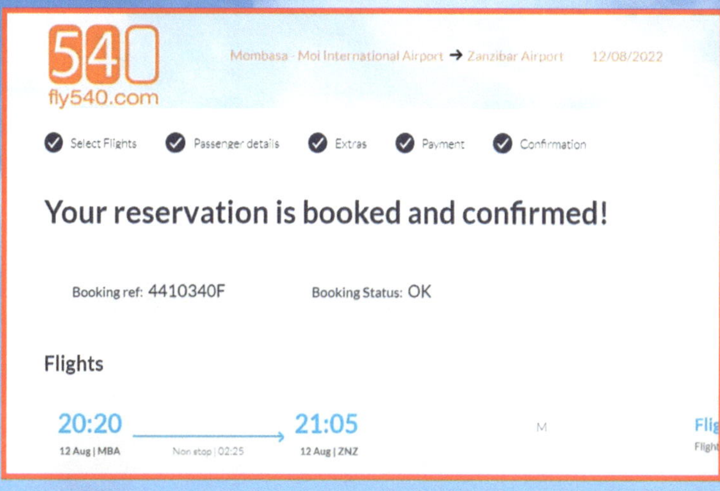

Ch 9 – 2022 First time visit to United Nations New York

During this particular milestone visit / trip to the UN in New York, we also attended a very special US / Africa TRADE summit. The invitation was received before laving Africa on our way back to the US.

During our milestone origin history time in ***Mombasa***, Kenya is where the trifecta MotherlandMade™ group was born – with. the. Kenyans, of course!!

MotherlandMade.com™
MotherlandMade.net™
MotherlandMade.org™

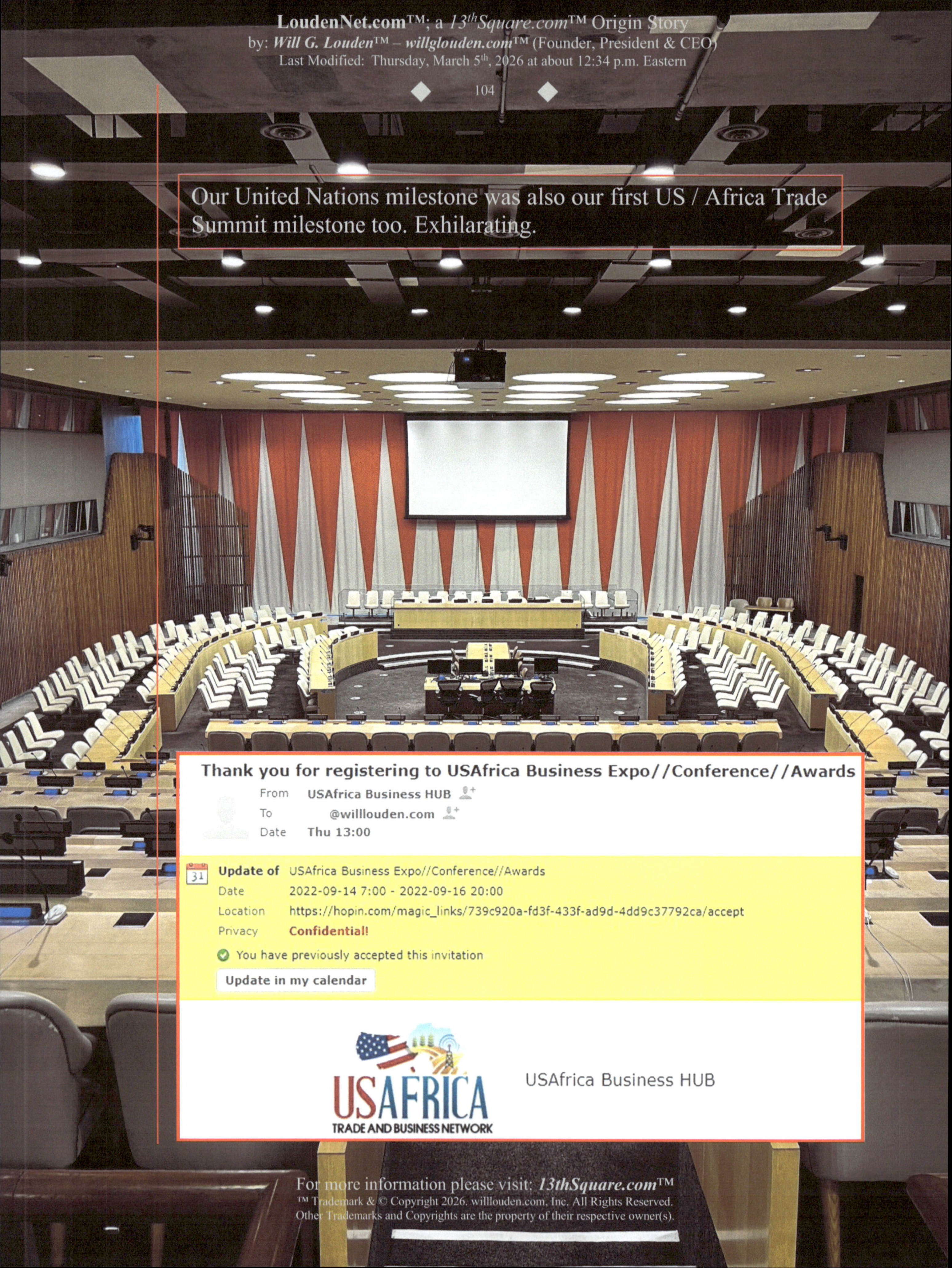

Our United Nations milestone was also our first US / Africa Trade Summit milestone too. Exhilarating.

Thank you for registering to USAfrica Business Expo//Conference//Awards

From USAfrica Business HUB
To @willlouden.com
Date Thu 13:00

Update of USAfrica Business Expo//Conference//Awards
Date 2022-09-14 7:00 - 2022-09-16 20:00
Location https://hopin.com/magic_links/739c920a-fd3f-433f-ad9d-4dd9c37792ca/accept
Privacy **Confidential!**

You have previously accepted this invitation

Update in my calendar

USAFRICA
TRADE AND BUSINESS NETWORK

USAfrica Business HUB

The African Union meeting space in New York.

Ch 9 – 2022 NJIT Capstone (PangeaSoul.com™) Student Team WINS Midterms

In 2022, our PangeaSoul.com™, NJIT Capstone student team WON, 1st place in the midterms!! That was a very exciting origin milestone; by the way, the below school top ranking picture, isn't associated with that WIN – it's simply background art.

Ch 9 – 2022 Sillicon Valley 1st Ever Conference and Visit

The milestone of us touching down in THE Valley, Silicon Valley, for the first time, to attend a high level, high stakes technology convention, that we were complimentary invited too…. Was. Simply: Enchanting!!

SAN JOSE McENERY CONVENTION CENTER
cruise
WELKOM
VELKOMMEN
ようこそ
Ground Transport

Richmond, Daly City 2
Exit
Milpitas
Elevator to Street
Milpitas

During this particular, initial milestone stop, "in the tech capital of the world," we mostly toured the urban centers and downtown San Francisco, California, USA. Later in this report / book we'll share another milestone stop, where we toured, the famous prison, Alcatraz, and several of the biggest tech companies on the planet!!

Chapter 10 (2024)

Origin Milestones

(24) 2024 Initial Cape Town Visit (January) | 33 African Nation RFP Became a Possibility | Plus 33 Nations Outside of Africa (Reality TV Show)

(25) 2024 Mobile App Developer Worldwide Publisher Rights (for the willlouden.com, Inc. company)
Google Playstore (February)
Apple App Store (March)

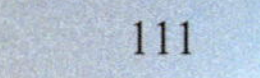

Ch 10 – 2024 Paramount Chief Security Officer Conference – New York

Before heading to Africa, in early 2024, we reached another milestone. This time it was a VIP invite only opportunity to meet and learn from some of the nations top security professionals at Paramount, in New York, USA.

Cal M
Chief Security Officer
S&P Global
55 Water Street, 37th floor
New York, NY 10041
T 212.438.
M
T (24/7)
@spglobal.com
spglobal.com
S&P Global

Ch 10 – 2024 First Time Touchdown in Cape Town, South Africa – RFP Movement

First off, Cape Town has some really nice beaches…

Before departing the US, this trip, bound for our first ever milestone trip to South Africa, the goal was to checkout the land, its people, facilities and infrastructure for a possible MotherlandMade.com™ First Trade Reality TV Show and Trade Convention. That plan was enhanced during this particular trip, we'll discuss that in a later milestone.

During our nearly two full months on the ground, we discovered a few of the finest things about the Cape Town experience; including Canal Walk, thanks to our very gracious hosts.

Cape Point

Cape Point, is a place where two major bodies of water meet and it's also breathtaking to say the least. During this initial trip to South Africa via Cape Town, life changing lessons were had. The whole entire Cape Town exploration allowed for greater plan and project clarity overall.

While in ***Cape Town***, checking things out, we happened across the path of several Africans from many other African nations attempting to make their way in South Africa. One of those meetings, in particular, was with a gentleman from the Congo – here we'll call him, "Congo Dude."

Congo Dude, liked our pending reality TV show and convention idea so well that he implored us to give other African nations a chance to host the planned events.

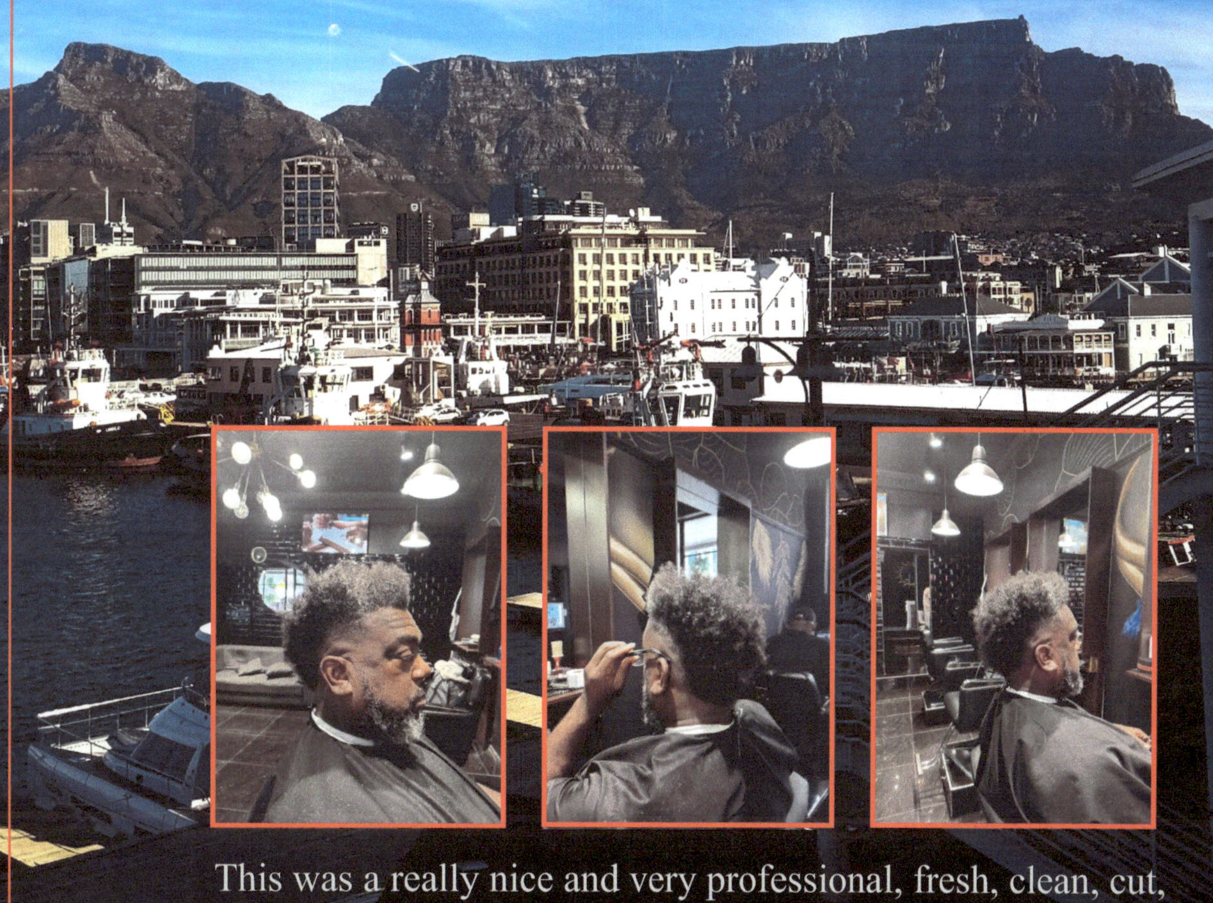

This was a really nice and very professional, fresh, clean, cut, received in the Cape Town Central Business District, by a young, "Zim" (Zimbabwe) gent. – MILESTONE!!

After meeting, "Congo Dude," while hanging out at a mall in Cape Town, where a subsequent meeting was eventually held and his sentiments gathered, we then made the decision to possibly explore a 33-African Nation RFP, combined with a potential 33-Nations external to Africa, eventually also participating in the potential Reality TV Show.

While visiting Cape Town, for the first time ever, we also visited the place / island where the globally respected and revered, ***President Nelson Mandela***, was held for twenty-seven years. It was another origin milestone and the source of inspiration for several of our other brands, products, services, and future events, etc.

There's no substitute for the knowledge, wisdom, and/or insights gained when speaking to and engaging natives.

willlouden.com, Inc.

Organization account Account ID:

Finish setting up your developer account

To publish apps on Google Play, finish setting up your developer account.

Google Play Console

Developer account created

We've sent a receipt for the registration fee to @gmail.com

Go to Play Console

The ***willlouden.com, Inc.***, Google and Apple, mobile app developer accounts, are likely two of our best origin milestones, ever. We respect both enterprises, immensely, and we're excited to have achieved these accomplishments!!

Continue your Apple Developer Program enrollment.

From **Apple Developer**
Date **Today 11:11**

Dear Will,

Your enrollment request has been accepted. You may now review the Program License Agreement to continue your organization's enrollment in the Apple Developer Program.

Review now.

Best regards,
Apple Developer Relations

PLEASE READ THE FOLLOWING APPLE DEVELOPER PROGRAM LICENSE AGREEMENT TERMS AND CONDITIONS CAREFULLY BEFORE DOWNLOADING OR USING THE APPLE SOFTWARE OR APPLE SERVICES. THESE TERMS AND CONDITIONS CONSTITUTE A LEGAL AGREEMENT BETWEEN YOU AND APPLE.

Apple Developer Program License Agreement

Purpose

You would like to use the Apple Software (as defined below) to develop one or more Applications (as defined below) for Apple-branded products. Apple is willing to grant You a limited license to use the Apple Software and Services provided to You under this Program to develop and test Your Applications on the terms and conditions set forth in this Agreement.

Chapter 11 (2024)

Origin Milestones

(26) 2024 Botswana Innovation Hub Visit (April) | Toured the Center; and Met its Government Director | Also Toured and met a Native Cell Phone Maker

(27) 2024 PejiAds.com™ Initial Advertising System Development NJIT Student Team PM Wins MVP (April)

Ch 11 – 2024 Initial Botswana, Africa Visit [Airport]

We first learned about the **Botswana Innovation Hub (BIH),** while watching an online video on a popular social media site. The online tour, interview, and presentation was so profound that we decided to schedule a stop in beautiful Botswana during our planned South Africa / Cape Town visit, and what a great decision.

BOTSWANA 50
BOTSWANA 50
BOTSWANA 50
BOTSWANA 50
HOME OF GENEROSITY
1256

WELCOME TO BOTSWANA
BOTSWANA
MUG & BEAN
AIR BOTSWANA
Tsodilo
REPUBLIC OF BOTSWANA

Ch 11 – 2024 Botswana Innovation Hub Visit [High Technology Incubator]

Ch 11 – 2024 Botswana Convention Hub Visit [Public Grand Gathering Place]

Ch 11 – 2024 NJIT Capstone Student Team Project Manager WINS MVP

NJIT – Full Page Picture

We understand that whenever a student and/or a, "student team," 'WINS,' it's largely due in part to their efforts. That said, we, too, rejoice and celebrate, all student team member WINS, as they are in fact, a very critical part of our overall and all encompassing global team, during an internship semester!! We count their milestones as our milestones, too, collectively.

Here, throughut our globally developing ecosystem, we're really just: one. big. happy. family, no matter how long the duration is for any one particular team member's stay.

Chapter 12 (2024)

Origin Milestones

(28) 2024 Gitex Africa Attendee; Moroccan King Invitee (May) | Also attended a Nigerian Wedding while there (Special Invite from the Mother of the Bride while at an Airport)

(29) 2024 1st Ever Virtual Phone Meeting with Google (August)

(30) 2024 NUBOE.COM Wyoming Company Formation (August)

Ch 12 – 2024 Gitex Africa Attendee; Moroccan King Invitee (May)

2024, was truly a magical year for us and our origin history. It's the year that we dropped down in Morocco, for the first time, to attend the biggest startup and tech conference, on the continent of Africa, by invitation of the King. This is clearly yet another, "crowning achievement," and/or milestone, if you will, in our development story!!

African Technical Treasure – wow

Extremely clean, and completely professional, are wonderful ways to describe this convention and the overall experience milestone as well. In all honestly, this was probably one of the classiest conventions that we've ever attended!!

GITEX
GLOBAL
GITEX
EUROPE
4 FEB 2025
AI EVERYTHING SUMMIT
5 - 6 FEB 2025
EXHIBITION SHOWCASE
EVERYTHING
GLOBAL
OCT 2024

Ch 12 – 2024 Nigerian Mother of the Bride Wedding Invitation – Moroccan Airport

After landing in Morocco, and while waiting to connect to the final destination airport, where the King's tech conference would be eventually held, we happened across the path of a, "Nigerian *Mother of the Bride*," who reached into her purse and invited us to a, 'Nigerian wedding,' slated for Morocco, on the spot!!

Mother of the Bride

They may have called this a, "wedding," and I'd imagine two people got married, but "this," was much more than a mere, 'wedding…' lol :_)

For us it was a fashion show, cultural presentation, and dance party all wrapped into one!!

It was an enchanting experience worthy of the, "*record books*!!"

Ch 12 – 2024 NUBOE.com and Google Cloud Virtual Connection Year

Google Calendar

Response has been saved.

✔ **Yes** Add a note or change response

Follow Up Nuboe - GCP

When	Thu Sep 12, 2024 9am – 9:30am Central Standard Time - Costa Rica
Joining info	meet.google.com/gve-vhqt-ift
	Or dial: +506 4010 2450 PIN: 1526334872790# More phone numbers
Calendar	@willlouden.com
Who	Yes: 2 No: 0 Maybe: 0 Waiting: 2 Optional: 0
	✔ @xwf.google.com - organizer
	✔ @willlouden.com
	@willlouden.com
	@google.com

In 2024, we also received a welcomed invitation from Google Cloud. This was, again, more than just a mere milestone, rather a surreal ***Bucket List*** level item?! ha.

Ch 12 – 2024 NUBOE.COM formed Under Wyoming Law

In August of 2024, after returning from Africa, and meeting with Google Cloud, for the first time ever, we made the ultimate decision to form, NUBOE.COM under Wyoming, USA law.

Received
AUG - 5 2024
Secretary of State
Wyoming

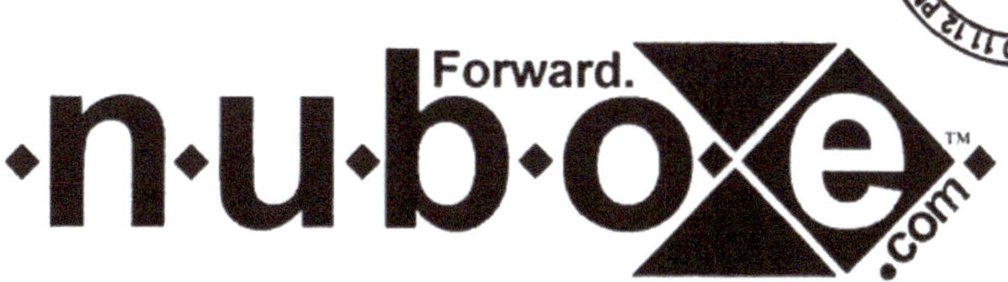

ARTICLES OF INCORPORATION OF

NUBOE.COM, INC.

A Wyoming Corporation

Chapter 13 (2024)

Origin Milestones

(31) 2024 "*Ground Floor*," Employment
Contract Book Complete (August)
Initial Team Members Join
Frank B. Officially Signs on too
Kenyan Leadership Team Joins
Initial NJIT Programmers Join

(32) 2024 JP Morgan Cap Table
Execution (September)

(33) 2024 Rite2Rule.com™ Domain
Acquired (September)

(34) 2024 Main Brands / Logos
Solidified

Ch 13 – 2024 Ground Floor; Employment Contract Book, COMPLETED.

Ground Floor; a *13thSquare.com*™ Employment Contract
by: ***Will G. Louden***™ – willglouden.com™ (Founder, President & CEO)
NUBOE.COM STAFF Stock Agreement, hereinafter STAFFSTKAGR
Last Date Modified: 9.28.24 @ 12:41 p.m. Eastern

Ground Floor;

a ***13th Square.com***™
Employment Contract

By: ***Will G. Louden***™ (***willglouden.com***™),
Founder / President / CEO

For more information please visit: ***13thSquare.com***™

Although, “Ground Floor,” is listed as an, “employment,” contract – the way its written and styled is more like that of a, “*partnership agreement*,” designed specifically for our initial sequence of mission critical stakeholder builders.

This is technically a book that is also a contract for our foundational stakeholder team members. This book spells out cash, equity, and various, award provisions, available under certain circumstances.

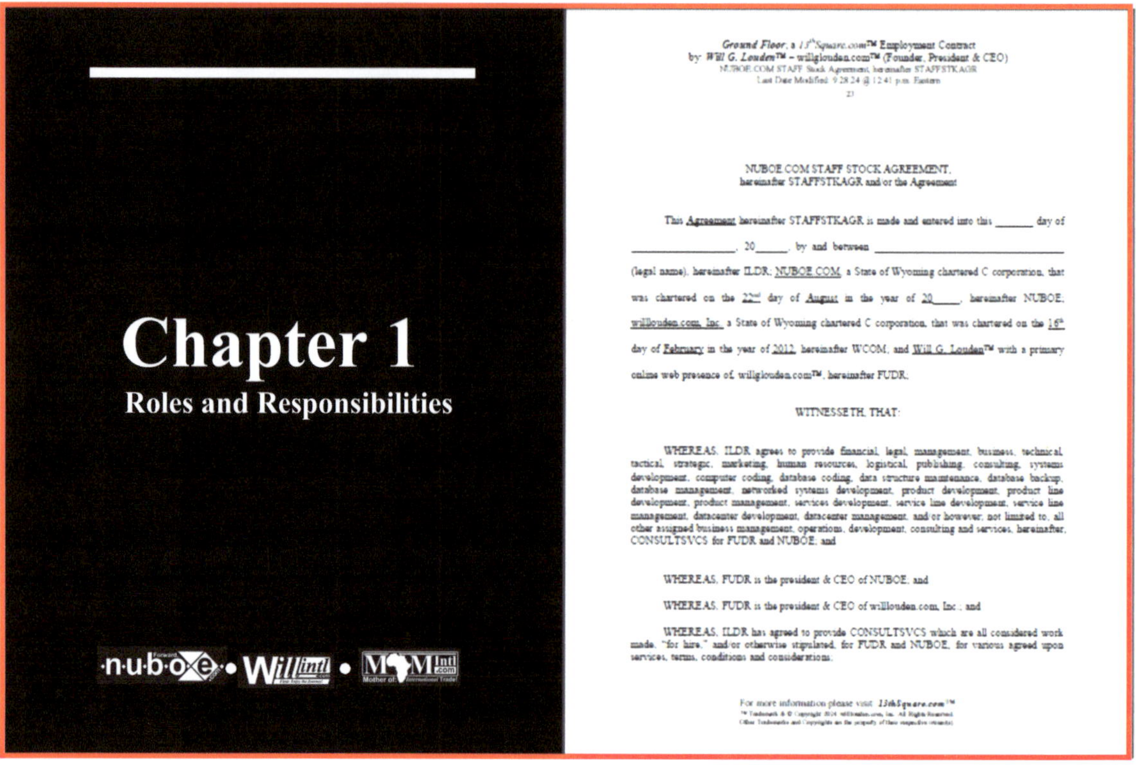

Ground Floor, a 13thSquare.com™ Employment Contract
by: *Will G. Louden*™ – willglouden.com™ (Founder, President & CEO)
NUBOE.COM STAFF Stock Agreement, hereinafter STAFFSTKAGR
Last Date Modified: 9.28.24 @ 12:41 p.m. Eastern
23

NUBOE.COM STAFF STOCK AGREEMENT,
hereinafter STAFFSTKAGR and/or the Agreement

This Agreement hereinafter STAFFSTKAGR is made and entered into this ______ day of ______________, 20_____, by and between ______________________________ (legal name), hereinafter ILDR; NUBOE.COM, a State of Wyoming chartered C corporation, that was chartered on the 22nd day of August in the year of 20____, hereinafter NUBOE; willlouden.com, Inc., a State of Wyoming chartered C corporation, that was chartered on the 16th day of February in the year of 2012, hereinafter WCOM; and Will G. Louden™ with a primary online web presence of, willglouden.com™, hereinafter FUDR;

WITNESSETH, THAT:

WHEREAS, ILDR agrees to provide financial, legal, management, business, technical, tactical, strategic, marketing, human resources, logistical, publishing, consulting, systems development, computer coding, database coding, data structure maintenance, database backup, database management, networked systems development, product development, product line development, product management, services development, service line development, service line management, datacenter development, datacenter management, and/or however, not limited to, all other assigned business management, operations, development, consulting and services, hereinafter, CONSULTSVCS for FUDR and NUBOE; and

WHEREAS, FUDR is the president & CEO of NUBOE; and

WHEREAS, FUDR is the president & CEO of willlouden.com, Inc.; and

WHEREAS, ILDR has agreed to provide CONSULTSVCS which are all considered work made, "for hire," and/or otherwise stipulated, for FUDR and NUBOE, for various agreed upon services, terms, conditions and considerations.

For more information please visit: *13thSquare.com*™

Ground Floor, a 13thSquare.com™ Employment Contract
by: *Will G. Louden*™ – willglouden.com™ (Founder, President & CEO)
NUBOE.COM STAFF Stock Agreement, hereinafter STAFFSTKAGR
Last Date Modified: 9.28.24 @ 12:41 p.m. Eastern

IN WITNESS WHEREOF, the parties hereto have caused this Agreement to be executed by their duly authorized officers and/or agents as of the day and year first above written.

____
willlouden.com, Inc., **Licensor**; by: Will G. Louden™ President / CEO

____
Will G. Louden™; **FUDR** President / CEO of NUBOE

____
NUBOE.COM; **Licensee**; by: Alexander M. Perlaza, Acting CFO

For more information please visit: *13thSquare.com*™

"Ground Floor," is a 13-chapter book. The chapters are generally, different agreements, company policies, and/or other material venture ***disclosures***, in the cases of the different developing brands, products, services, events and/or initiatives, etc. etc.

These are base chapters that are used in other books that also serve the ventures growing stakeholder base. Other books that are based on this book may have additional chapters, at the end and/or replacement chapters, which may also include many of these base chapters.

In as much as it's a, "relationship tool," *Ground Floor*, is also a bit of a, 'marketing tool,' as well, because in it are many visionary blueprint elements, too. Yes, there are various material disclosures, but there are also elements of, Ground Floor marketing strategies found within as well.

The disclosure of BRANDS helps to paint a picture of whom we are and where we're going.

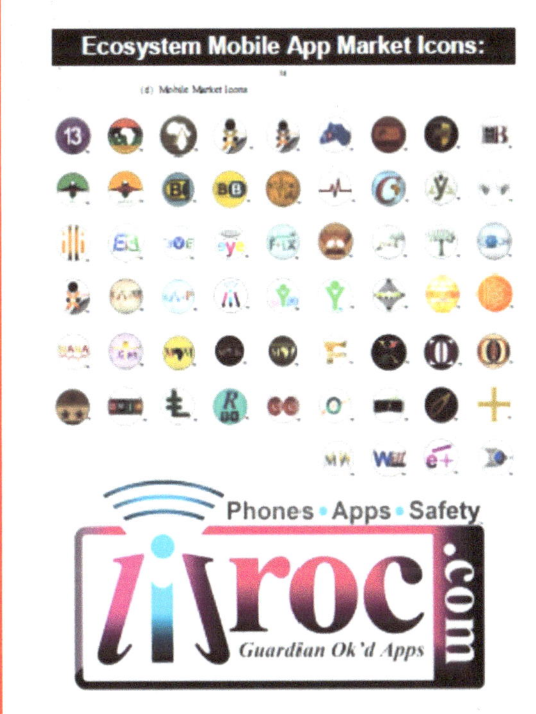

The completion of, "Ground Floor," was a tremendous origin milestone and a true accomplishment for us because it became the legal underpinning, "tool" needed to help us firm up several key stakeholder deals and relationships.

In this book / contract / disclosure and marketing guide, etc. we even talk about our now and future strategic global operating structures.

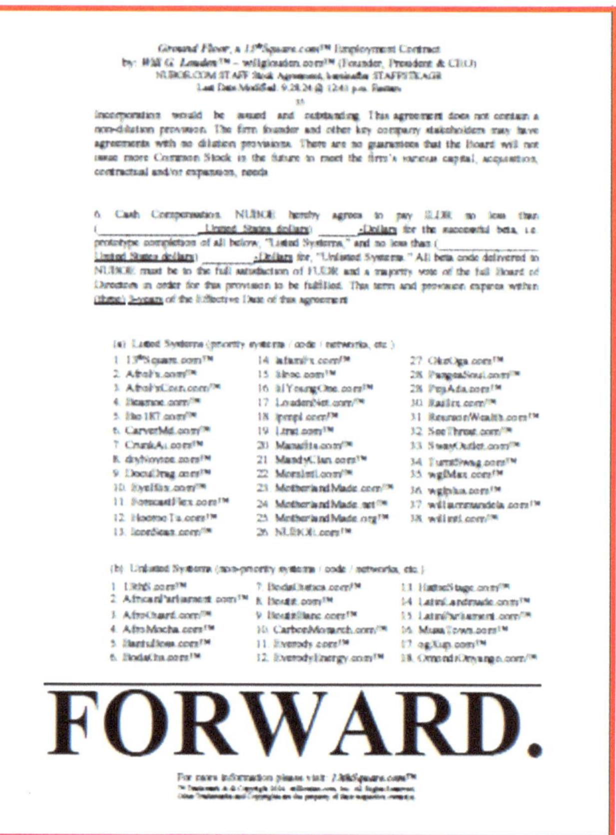

Ground Floor, a 13thSquare.com™ Employment Contract
by: *Will G. Louden™* – willglouden.com™ (Founder, President & CEO)
NUBOE.COM STAFF Stock Agreement, hereinafter STAFFSTKAGR
Last Date Modified: 9.28.24 @ 12:41 p.m. Eastern
35

Incorporation would be issued and outstanding. This agreement does not contain a non-dilution provision. The firm founder and other key company stakeholders may have agreements with no dilution provisions. There are no guarantees that the Board will not issue more Common Stock in the future to meet the firm's various capital, acquisition, contractual and/or expansion, needs.

6. Cash Compensation. NUBOE hereby agrees to pay [illegible] no less than (__________ United States dollars) ______-Dollars for the successful beta, i.e. prototype completion of all below, "Listed Systems," and no less than (__________ United States dollars) ______-Dollars for, "Unlisted Systems." All beta code delivered to NUBOE must be to the full satisfaction of [illegible] and a majority vote of the full Board of Directors in order for this provision to be fulfilled. This term and provision expires within (three) 3-years of the Effective Date of this agreement.

(a) Listed Systems (priority systems / code / networks, etc.)

1. 13thSquare.com™	14. [illegible].com™	27. [illegible].com™
2. [illegible].com™	15. [illegible].com™	28. PangeaSoul.com™
3. [illegible].com™	16. [illegible]YoungOne.com™	29. [illegible].com™
4. Beamoe.com™	17. LoudenNet.com™	30. [illegible].com™
5. [illegible].com™	18. [illegible].com™	31. ReunionWealth.com™
6. CarverMd.com™	19. [illegible].com™	32. [illegible].com™
7. CrunkAi.com™	20. Manafits.com™	33. [illegible]Outlet.com™
8. [illegible].com™	21. MandyClan.com™	34. TurntSwag.com™
9. [illegible].com™	22. [illegible].com™	35. wglMax.com™
10. [illegible].com™	23. MotherlandMade.com™	36. wglplus.com™
11. ForecastFlex.com™	24. MotherlandMade.net™	37. [illegible].com™
12. [illegible].com™	25. MotherlandMade.org™	38. willintl.com™
13. [illegible].com™	26. NUBOE.com™	

(b) Unlisted Systems (non-priority systems / code / networks, etc.)

1. [illegible].com™	7. [illegible].com™	13. [illegible]Stage.com™
2. AfricanParliament.com™	8. [illegible].com™	14. [illegible].com™
3. AfroGuard.com™	9. [illegible].com™	15. [illegible]Parliament.com™
4. AfroMocha.com™	10. CarbonMonarch.com™	16. [illegible].com™
5. [illegible].com™	11. Everody.com™	17. ogXup.com™
6. [illegible].com™	12. EverodyEnergy.com™	18. [illegible].com™

FORWARD.

NUBOE.COM™ is our (VERY) tentative global primary Intellectual Property Supreme Licensing Company…

WillIntl.com™ is our (VERY) tentative, U.S. and "Americas," primary Supreme Management Company…

MOMIntl.com™ is our (VERY) tentative, Africa and "the World," primary Supreme Management Company…

(c) Developing Brands

Ground Floor, a 13thSquare.com™ Employment Contract
by: *Will G. Louden™* – willglouden.com™ (Founder, President & CEO)
NUBOX.COM STAFF Book Agreement, hereinafter STAFFBKAGR
Last Date Modified: 9.28.24 @ 12:41 p.m. Eastern

2. Licensee hereby agrees to indemnify and hold harmless Licensor and its directors, officers and employees from any and/or all claims of a third party arising out of and/or in connection with any claim that Licensee use of the Licensed Trademarks violates the rights of such third party to such Licensed Trademarks.

Article 8 – Miscellaneous

1. Entire Agreement. This Agreement (including the Schedule constituting a part of this Agreement) and any other writing signed by the parties that specifically references this Agreement constitute the entire agreement among the parties with respect to the subject matter hereof and supersede all prior agreements, understandings and/or negotiations, both written and oral, between the parties with respect to the subject matter hereof. This Agreement is not intended to confer upon any Person other than the parties hereto any rights and/or remedies hereunder.

2. Assign-ability. This Agreement may not be assigned nor transferred by Licensee without the prior written, signed and notarized consent of Licensor.

3. Extension of Rights. All rights and obligations incurred hereunder by Licensee shall extend to and be binding upon their respective domestic and international divisions, subsidiaries, affiliates, other controlled companies, brands, divisions, managed enterprises, managed brands, associated affiliates and/or related entities.

4. Waiver. The waiver by Licensor of a breach of any provision contained herein shall be in writing and shall in no way be construed as a waiver of any subsequent breach of such provision or the waiver of the provision itself.

5. Injunctive Relief. Licensee hereby acknowledges that monetary relief would not be an adequate remedy for a breach and/or any threatened breach of the provisions of this Agreement and that Licensor shall be entitled to the enforcement of this Agreement by injunction, specific performance and/or any other equitable relief, without prejudice to any other rights and/or remedies that Licensor has and/or may have.

6. Disclaimer of Agency, Partnership and/or Joint Venture. Nothing in this Agreement, except in agreements, circumstances and/or situations where explicitly written, shall constitute and/or be deemed to constitute a partnership and/or joint venture between the parties hereto and/or constitute and/or be deemed to constitute

For more information please visit: *13thSquare.com™*

Ground Floor, a 13thSquare.com™ Employment Contract
by: *Will G. Louden™* – willglouden.com™ (Founder, President & CEO)
NUBOX.COM STAFF Book Agreement, hereinafter STAFFBKAGR
Last Date Modified: 9.28.24 @ 12:41 p.m. Eastern

any party to the agent and/or employee of the other party for any purpose whatsoever and neither party shall have authority and/or power to bind the other and/or to contract in the name of and/or create a liability against the other in any way and/or for any purpose.

7. Severability. If any provision of this Agreement shall be held as invalid and/or unenforceable, then such invalidity and/or unenforceability shall not render the entire Agreement invalid. Rather, the Agreement shall be construed as if not containing that particular invalid and/or unenforceable part and/or provision and any surviving rights and/or obligations of each party shall be construed and enforced accordingly.

8. Official Notices. All notices are to be sent to the parties as spelled out in the "Roles and Responsibilities," section 4 of this book and/or STAFFBKAGR.

9. Arbitration. Any controversy and/or claim arising hereunder that cannot be resolved by the parties themselves, shall be settled by binding arbitration, in accordance with the Commercial Arbitration Rules of the American Arbitration Association. Any award rendered thereon shall be in writing and shall be final and binding on the parties and judgment may be entered thereon in any court of competent jurisdiction. Each party shall bear its own costs and expenses in connection with the arbitration and the costs and expenses of the arbitrators shall be borne as determined by the arbitrator.

For more information please visit: *13thSquare.com™*

Also, while many of these initial agreements, all in fact, were executed / (signed) in a PDF online execution fashion, we have plans and systems in place, in house, to expedite document imaging, encoding, storage, retrieval, and management systems processing – the ecosystem brand for us is the: DocuDrag.com™ platform.

The ability to execute documents, online, will help us scale, Fast!! – Worldwide!

Online Document Management and Execution = Ease of Compliance!!

In some ways, many in fact, the *Ground Floor* work, is also a bit of an origin story.

There are many instances sprinkled throughout the work, which shed light on our past, present, and future – and also some of what makes us, us and why we do the things that we do, etc.

Building, empowering, and uplifting people and communities is simply apart of our DNA!!

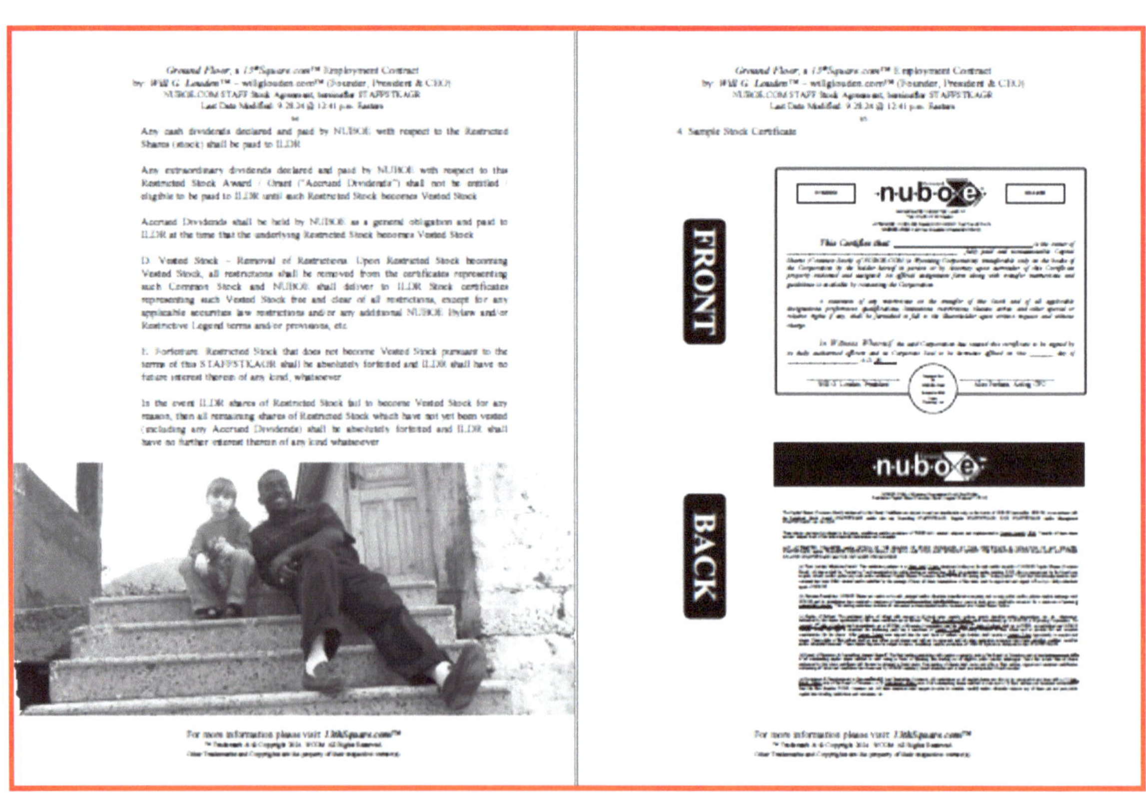

Ground Floor; a *13thSquare.com™* Employment Contract
by: *Will G. Louden™* – willglouden.com™ (Founder, President & CEO)
NUBOE.COM STAFF Stock Agreement, hereinafter STAFFSTKAGR
Last Date Modified: 9.28.24 @ 12:41 p.m. Eastern

Any cash dividends declared and paid by NUBOE with respect to the Restricted Shares (stock) shall be paid to ILDR.

Any extraordinary dividends declared and paid by NUBOE with respect to this Restricted Stock Award / Grant ("Accrued Dividends") shall not be entitled / eligible to be paid to ILDR until such Restricted Stock becomes Vested Stock.

Accrued Dividends shall be held by NUBOE as a general obligation and paid to ILDR at the time that the underlying Restricted Stock becomes Vested Stock.

D. Vested Stock – Removal of Restrictions. Upon Restricted Stock becoming Vested Stock, all restrictions shall be removed from the certificates representing such Common Stock and NUBOE shall deliver to ILDR Stock certificates representing such Vested Stock free and clear of all restrictions, except for any applicable securities law restrictions and/or any additional NUBOE Bylaw and/or Restrictive Legend terms and/or provisions, etc.

E. Forfeiture. Restricted Stock that does not become Vested Stock pursuant to the terms of this STAFFSTKAGR shall be absolutely forfeited and ILDR shall have no future interest therein of any kind, whatsoever.

In the event ILDR shares of Restricted Stock fail to become Vested Stock for any reason, then all remaining shares of Restricted Stock which have not yet been vested (including any Accrued Dividends) shall be absolutely forfeited and ILDR shall have no further interest therein of any kind whatsoever.

Ground Floor; a *13thSquare.com™* Employment Contract
by: *Will G. Louden™* – willglouden.com™ (Founder, President & CEO)
NUBOE.COM STAFF Stock Agreement, hereinafter STAFFSTKAGR
Last Date Modified: 9.28.24 @ 12:41 p.m. Eastern

4. Sample Stock Certificate

FRONT

nuboxe

BACK

nuboxe

Nobue <> Cap Tables by JP Morgan Workplace Solutions

From Conor
To @willglouden.com, @willlouden.com
Date 29.08.2024 15:29

Pleasure meeting you both just now, Will & Alex,

As promised, please find enclosed our platform pdf one-pager. Hopefully this will serve useful moving forward.

And to recap some of today's talking points:

- The solution is complementary for companies with less than stakeholders.
- Included is complementary concierge onboarding and customer success support.
- Once a company surpasses the stakeholder threshold, it is per stakeholder per month, billed annually – inclusive of all stakeholders.

Looking forward to hearing back from you once you have spoken internally.

Kind regards,
Conor.

Employing, *JP Morgan Workplace Solutions*, as the 'exclusive,' NUBOE.COM, equity ledger partner, is very likely, one of our best decisions yet. The process was an eye opener, to be sure. We preformed extensive research before making this decision.

After a few meetings, time, and research, etc., we made the decision to go with JPM, for a variety of reasons. Their solution serves our enterprise incredibly well and we're more than happy (and grateful in fact) to have them on board!

Ground Floor, also mentions brands, services, industry's and markets where we operate and plan to enter in the future. Two, in particular are market exchanges – one serving Africa and the other serving Latin America. Grateful.

NUBOE.COM || 30 N. Gould || Sheridan, WY 82801
Home of the *Gold Star VIP* Hardback Book Covers

Memorandum

To:	Conor @jpmorgan.com
Cc:	Rena with JPMorgan Solutions Team @jpmchase.com jpmorgan.com
From:	Will G. Louden™ President / CEO
Cc:	Alexander Perlaza, Acting CFO Frank & Global Tech Team
Date:	Friday, September 6th, 2024
Re:	Cap Tables by J.P. Morgan – NUBOE.COM

Conor:

Alex and I were incredibly pleased and impressed with your presentation and capital table solution for small businesses like ours. The complimentary services also caught our attention!! To that end, this morning, we concluded our 409A and capital table preliminary research with an outstanding meeting with Fidelity.

It was a tough race but a decision had to be made!! ***Congratulations***; NUBOE.COM is very interested in any and/or all next steps relative to test driving your services as a bona fide capital table client. :_)

How might this best be accomplished?! Also, is there a contract that we can review?!

Thank you again for spending the time with us and for sharing your outstanding small business capital table solutions; we sincerely appreciate it!!

Best Regards!!

Ch 13 – 2024 NUBOE.com Ecosystem Main Brands Cover Finalized

MANAfits.com™ More than Benefits. Manafits.
LPMd.com
Life People Money People Life
Aglmax.com™
Musa Town .com – A Royal Light House – Prosperity Smart City Limits Illuminated!
HattieStage.com™
MotherLANMade.NET – Leadership Africa Network
PangeaSoul.com™
wglplus.com™ – Watch. Game. Learn. Plus+
TurntSwag.com™ – Your FinTech Wallet.
AfricanParliament.com™ – UNITY: THE Road to Freedom.
diyNovice.com™ – Doing. Life. Your. Way!!
ForecastFlex.com™ – Financial Empowerment. By Store. By Region.
William Mandela™
PangeaSoul '22 WORLD TOUR™
AfroGUARD.com™ – Guarding the Peace.
DocuDrag.com™ – Paperless Cloud Storage
13thSquare.com™ – Knowledge on Demand.
BoutitBanc.com™
OmondiOnyango™ – A Birth at Dawn. Rising Son.
EVErody.com™
afroFXCOIN.com™ – 1Market. 1People. Many Products. 1Coin.
MotherlandMade .com .net .org™
Afro MOCHA .com™
Podcasts + LOUDENNET.com™ – Hosting Data Domains
LatinLandMade.com – Final Production: South America.
eyeblix.com™ – Your Voice Worldwide.
willlouden.com™
MANAfits™ – More than Benefits. Manafits.
EVErodyEnergy.com™
Bio187.com™ – Be a Killa.
SWAYOutlet.com™
ReunionWealth.com™ – Health • Capital • Unity
CarbonMonarch.com™ – Eye. Your. Crown. – Royal Level Service: DELIVERED.
pejiAds.com™ – Broad Range. Tremendous Reach.
13thS.com™ – Publishing.
bodaGIS.com™ – LOVE Delivered
lafamFX.com™ – One Market.
MotherlandMade.org™ – Champions Aid Africa
MandyClan.com™ – We. Are. One.
willlouden.com
WILLIAMMANDELA™ – Will: I. Am. Mandela.
CrunkAi.com™ – Accelerated Innovation
GordenAbson.com™
bodaGIStics.com™
FFX™ – Financial Empowerment – By Store. By Region. By You.
CarNerMd.com™ – Virtual Health Delivered
Boutit.com™ – Real Estate
WillIntl.com™ – First: Enjoy the Journey!
LatinParliament™ – UNITY: THE Road to Freedom.com
lilYoungOne.com™ – Growing in Knowledge.
MOMIntl.com™ – Mother of: International Trade!
OGXUp.com™ – Keep Climbing.
OkeOga.com™
iiroc.com™ – Phones • Apps • Safety – Who's Calling You?
nuboe.com™ – Forward.
afroFX.com™ – One Market.
Beamoe.com™ – Text. Voice. Email. +
ICONSean.com™
hoorooTu.com™ – From the Root to the WORLD: HoorooTu Country Manager
raillix.com™
Ltrat.com™ – Payments+
BantuBOSS.com™ – Premium Luxury. Extraordinary Achievement.
hoorooTu™ – From the Root to the WORLD: HoorooTu Country Manager
SeeTHREAT.com™ – Mitigating: Risk of Loss.
MotherlandMade.com™ – Final Production: Africa
TurntSwag™ – Your FinTech Wallet.

Chapter 14 (2024)

Origin Milestones

(35) 2024 2nd Trip out to Silicon Valley
(Sponsor: API: World) (November)
Facebook Campus Visit
Google Campus Visit
Apple Campus Visit

Ch 14 – 2024 Silicon Valley Visit [External Facebook Campus Tour]

Facebook

Facebook – Both Pictures

In addition to attending a very special API conference, that took us out to THE Valley, in late 2024, we also toured three of the biggest high tech company headquarters, including: (1) Facebook, (2) Apple and (3) Google – it was all such avery special treat; We also dropped by Stanford and Berkley, too, and spent almost a full, if not half day, at the legendary albeit formidable, ***Alcatraz Prison***.

All of these were origin milestones and defining moments, and the absolute trip of a lifetime for the record books, for sure!! wow.

Facebook – Full Page Picture
API: World – Small Picture

You're Invited -- The API World + CloudX 2024 Hackathon (Oct 21-Nov 7)

Ch 14 – 2024 Silicon Valley Visit [External Google Campus Tour]

Google

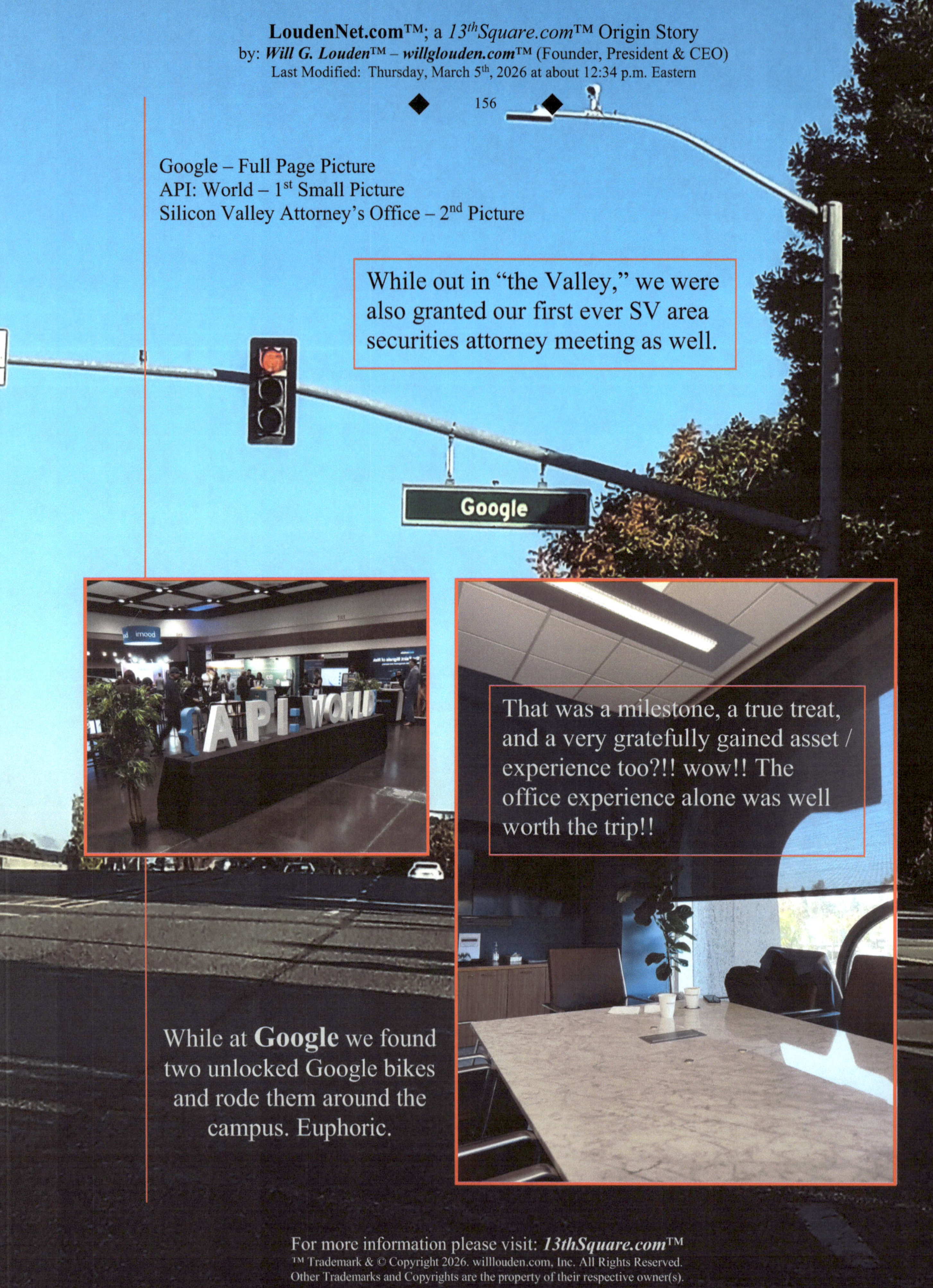

Google – Full Page Picture
API: World – 1st Small Picture
Silicon Valley Attorney's Office – 2nd Picture

While out in "the Valley," we were also granted our first ever SV area securities attorney meeting as well.

That was a milestone, a true treat, and a very gratefully gained asset / experience too?!! wow!! The office experience alone was well worth the trip!!

While at **Google** we found two unlocked Google bikes and rode them around the campus. Euphoric.

Ch 14 – 2024 Silicon Valley Visit [External Apple Campus Tour]

Apple

Apple – Full Page Picture
API: World – Smaller Picture
iPhone 16 Pro
API:WORLD

Apple – Full Page Picture
Stanford – 2 Smaller Pictures

For more information please visit: ***13thSquare.com™***

Chapter 15 (2025)

Origin Milestones

(36) 2025 Trump Washington DC Victory Ball Invitee (January) | Received Invite while Preparing to Fly Back to Africa

(37) 2025 Africa Third Continental Visit (February) | Nigeria, Africa Visit (February to March)

Ch 15 – 2025 President Trump Washington, DC Victory Ball Invite

Join us in Washington, DC on January 19 & 20, 2025 for a celebration of historic proportions!

TRUMP VICTORY CELEBRATION BALL – January 19, 2025
Indulge in a formal dinner and grand celebration honoring the victory. Mingle with members of the incoming administration, conservative media, and some of the greatest leaders of our time.

Victory Ball Agenda
4:15 PM Arrival
4:45 PM Reception
6:00 PM Formal Dinner

VIP Tickets Available – Ask Now!

PRESIDENT TRUMP'S INAUGURATION – January 20
Be part of history in the making as we witness President Donald J. Trump's inauguration on the steps of the Capitol.

PATRIOTS UNITE!
ON JANUARY 19 & 20, 2025 IN WASHINGTON, DC

Exclusive Private Invitation

Congratulations President Trump

American Freedom Tour
Trump Victory Ball
In Celebration of the Inauguration of our 47th President
January 19, 2025

&

Inauguration of *President Donald J. Trump*
January 20, 2025

Politics aside, once elected, leaders are leaders, no matter what our individual political leanings?!

That said, receiving a head of state, 'ball invite,' is to be considered another welcomed milestone?!!

Ch 15 – 2025 Lagos, Nigeria – Africa first ever Visit [February to March 27 Days]

Visas

First off, the process of obtaining a, "Nigerian VISA," was extensive and expensive (lol) but worth it?! The journey began by applying online but continued upon discovering that a requirement to travel to a, "Nigerian biometric center," was also required. The place of choice was in New York, which added considerable costs to the whole entire visa acquisition costs, but upon completion, the 5-year multiple entry VISA, was well welcomed, not only as a well achieved milestone, but also as a tool for helping to position and advance our continental business interests. The ***first class*** flight over was also an absolute treat!!

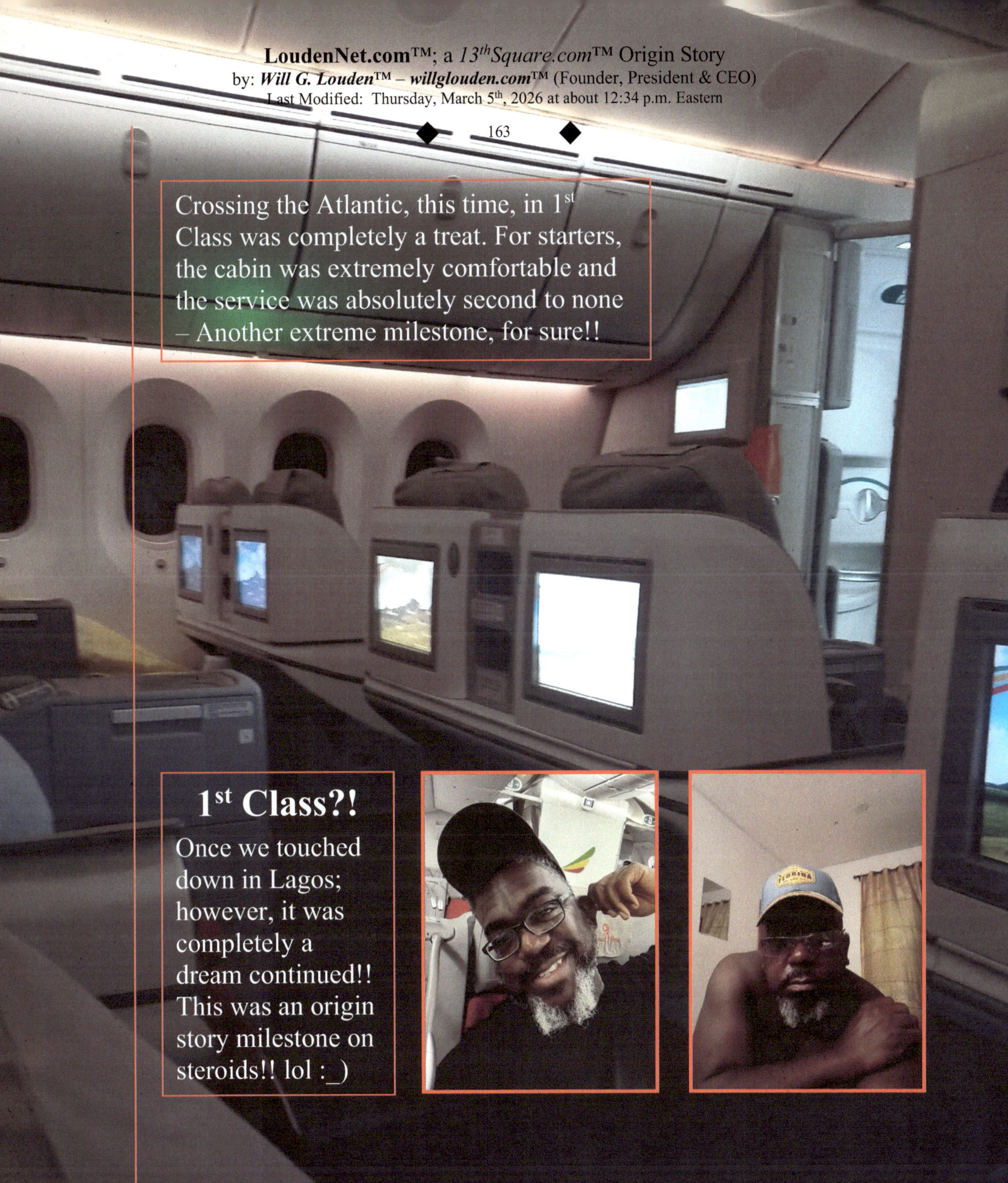

Crossing the Atlantic, this time, in 1st Class was completely a treat. For starters, the cabin was extremely comfortable and the service was absolutely second to none – Another extreme milestone, for sure!!

1st Class?!

Once we touched down in Lagos; however, it was completely a dream continued!! This was an origin story milestone on steroids!! lol :_)

While in Lagos we traveled to the ***University of Ibadan***, by invitation of a very well respected and connected, Nigerian / US businessman; it's the same guy who invited us to the USAfrica Trade summit at the UN back in 2022.

For more information please visit: ***13thSquare.com***™

Once in Lagos, our primarily travel was by bus, bike and walk(ing)!!

Actually, on our way to / from Lagos we passed through Ivory Coast.

One evening, we dined at THE **Black Diamond Hotel**. Actually, it was recommended to us by one of our many rideshare drivers, while transitioning in-between cities. We took his advice and checked the hotel out one night and the rest is history!!

Skywalk Right of Passage

A highlight and true delight of Lagos is / was the ***Nature Conversancy***.

Lekki Beach / Lagos.
NO. WORDS. NEEDED.

This particular origin milestone completed our visit to several of Africa's most treasured coasts. Previous, to this visit, we visited Mombasa Beach, in Kenya, on the East Coast of Africa and Cape Town Beach in South Africa on the Southern Coast… There's nothing like a trifecta, right?! lol :_) MILESTONES.

Chapter 16 (2025)

Origin Milestones

(38) 2025 ForecastFlex.com™ NJIT Student Team Places 3rd (April) | Team Project Manager Wins MVP for the Semester

(39) 2025 First Ever Pretoria, South Africa Visit (March to May) | Chief Legal Officer Joins

ForecastFlex.com™
Financial Empowerment. By Store. By Region.

In the Spring of 2025, our ForecastFlex.com™ NJIT Capstone, student team, WON 3rd place and that team's project manager, WON – MVP!! CONGRATULATIONS! We consider it yet another collective origin story WIN too!

Ch 16 – 2025 Arrival in Pretoria, South Africa Mission Exploration

Pretoria, South Africa, is surprisingly beautiful. This; however, is a shot from the Penthouse balcony, in Johannesburg. These are/were simply stunning and amazing views. The mosquitoes still bite though even from this level – lol haha.

The visit to Pretoria, South Africa, was our first, but it was also a trip filled with precise luxury and wonder.

For more information please visit: ***13thSquare.com***™

YOU JUST BECAME
A LEGEND.

While in Pretoria, we met some of the most intelligent, hospitable and kind Africans, that one would ever want to meet. One in particular, was a well informed lawyer, who saw and caught the ecosystem vision, and made the right decision to officially (and formally) sign on, as our brand spanking new, Chief Legal Officer.

We're glad to have him aboard to help BUILD – this is yet another incredible origin milestone to which we are extremely proud and grateful!

In Pretoria and in Sandton, the food, ambiance, entertainment and night life was completely and absolutely, **World Class**!! And to have experienced it all, in grand fashion, during the summer while going into fall, is just one more testament to our origins and various operational milestones of excellence and diplomacy!!

WORLD CLASS.

(40) Initial NUBOE.COM Board of Directors Established

(41) 2025 First Ever Visit to PayPal Manhattan (NY) Offices

(42) Byte Knights Established

Chapter 17 (2025)

Origin Milestones

(43) Rite2Rule.com™ Underway (June)

(44) "Ground Floor R2R," Published

(45) SeeThreat.com™ MVP Complete

(46) PejiAds.com™ Dev. Continues

(47) HoorooTu.com™ Dev. Begins

(48) "*Hollywood*," Talent Contract Book Commences Production (July)

Ch 17 – 2025 NUBOE.COM Initial Board of Directors Established

NUBOE.COM || 30 N. Gould || Sheridan, WY 82801
Home of the *Gold Star VIP* Hardback Book Covers

Special Board Member Appointment

Date: Monday, June 23rd, 2025
To: Newly Appointed Initial Board Members
From: ***Will G. Louden***™ Founder / Chairman

wow. CONGRATULATIONS and WELCOME to the initial, NUBBOE.COM, Board of Directors!! Thank you for contributing to our growing multinational venture!!

This starter board will help to scale and approve any number of things relative to our growing enterprise, including, at some point, even possibly, nominating a more seasoned replacement and longer-term board in the future; for now; however, your term will be for one year or less. Some seats may be replaced as we enter and complete the pending SeeThreat.com™ Friends and Family round as well as our eventual initial cash capital round too; nevertheless and for now, ***Welcome Aboard***!!

Also, heads up, please plan to meet in-person later in the year when I'm scheduled to fly to and/or back from Europe; I'm scheduled to enter and depart the country through a New York area airport so be on the lookout for greater clarity before then (dates, time and place is forthcoming). Most of our meetings will be virtual but this initial meeting should be symbolically: ***in-person***?!

For Now these are the Tentative Initial Members:
1) Will G. Louden™ Founder / Chairman / CEO
2) Frank B. None Executive Board Vice Chairman
3) Alex P. Sr. VP, Chief Knowledge Officer (Secretary)
4) Duane H. Sr. VP, Chief Operating Officer
5) *Raymond L. Chief Technology Officer
6) Madumetja M. Sr. VP, Chief Legal Officer (Attorney)
7) Nirmal R. Sr. VP, Chief Security Officer
8) William D. Sr. VP, Chief People Officer

In December of 2012, right after the President was reelected, we received another surprised invitation from the Governor of the state of Arkansas, to attend the annual, "Christmas party." It was a completely euphoric moment and milestone. Here, we pose with the interns.

Ch 17 – 2025 First Ever Visit to PayPal Manhattan (New York, USA) Offices

Also in 2025:

- Byte Knights Team Established
- Rite2Rule.com™ Underway

In 2025, upon landing back in America, from another amazing trip / journey to Africa, we were invited to an event at, PayPal!!

EXIT
AVAN gallery
AVANT gallery
LOV

Ch 17 – 2025 Ground Floor R2R Published Worldwide on Amazon.com

So we've not just been traveling the world and living it up, on the contrary, upon returning from Africa and making a quick pit stop in New York, to visit PayPal, we flew on down to Miami to attend an invite only Crypto event, at a super swanky Miami Art Gallery…

After returning from Africa, we also got to work publishing the public vcrsion of thc, “Ground Floor,” work. It’s the same book as previously completed, well almost, with a few key changes. The book omits actual contract term values as used in actual team member agreements. The book also removes several pictures of the founder and replaces those pictures with a few of the most stunning shots from all around South Africa.

Two versions of this public work were published. One version is the black and white, low cost paperback version, while the other is a slightly higher end, “gold signature,” full color, hard cover version. This is the cover for that particular version of the published work.

The Rite2Rule.com™ platform is a place where practically all stakeholders will voice their various sentiments, from board voting, to shareholder voting, to even public and department / group team member voting, etc. – all of such group engagement and consensus will be handled by and/or through this particular platform.

This is part of the reason why the, "R2R," was added to the end of the officially published title and version of the original, "Ground Floor," work. For the most part, they are the exact same book, with cosmetic exceptions. This move really is to signify that it's not only a different book, but that it's also all about Democracy, in "OUR" ecosystem!!

Rite2Rule.com™ is a private, sometimes paid, membership platform serving practically the entire NUBOE.COM global ecosystem of managed products and services. It's the place where you can join and vote on particular issues placed before our community of supporters. It's also a place where we intend to offer our best deals and specials, too, if you will. It's also a bit of a ***fan club*** for those who support our team of *rock star builders and developers* including the firm founder: ***Will G. Louden™*** (***willglouden.com™***).

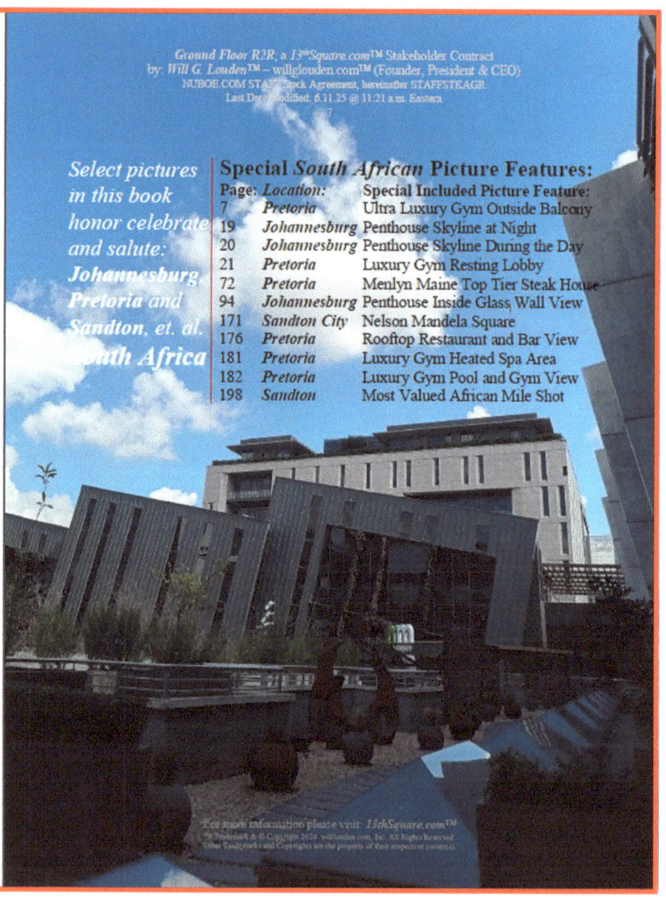

Ground Floor R2R; a *13thSquare.com™* Stakeholder Contract
by: *Will G. Louden™* – willglouden.com™ (Founder, President & CEO)
NUBOE.COM STAFF Stock Agreement, hereinafter STAFFSTKAGR
Last Date Modified: 6.11.25 @ 11:21 a.m. Eastern
7

Select pictures in this book honor celebrate and salute: ***Johannesburg, Pretoria and Sandton, et. al. South Africa***

Special *South African* Picture Features:

Page:	***Location:***	**Special Included Picture Feature:**
7	*Pretoria*	Ultra Luxury Gym Outside Balcony
19	*Johannesburg*	Penthouse Skyline at Night
20	*Johannesburg*	Penthouse Skyline During the Day
21	*Pretoria*	Luxury Gym Resting Lobby
72	*Pretoria*	Menlyn Maine Top Tier Steak House
94	*Johannesburg*	Penthouse Inside Glass Wall View
171	*Sandton City*	Nelson Mandela Square
176	*Pretoria*	Rooftop Restaurant and Bar View
181	*Pretoria*	Luxury Gym Heated Spa Area
182	*Pretoria*	Luxury Gym Pool and Gym View
198	*Sandton*	Most Valued African Mile Shot

For more information please visit: *13thSquare.com™*

Typically, but not always, whenever the word, "Gold," appears at the end of a title, it signifies that the work is the hardback / full color version of another work.

Why offer multiple formats?

Ground Floor R2R: a 13thSquare.com

Paperback
LIVE

$19.98 USD
View on Amazon
…N: 1637624344

Live

Your title is live on Amazon and is available for purchase. To learn more about ordering Author Copies click here.

Print Previewer

Ground Floor R2R Gold
Authored by Will G. Louden

Hardcover
Case Laminate

NUBOE is not required to specifically set aside assets to insure THEIPLAN performance. Neither WCOM, NUBOE, the Board and or FUDR shall be required to guarantee absolutely any Plan performance beyond any term and/or condition of an Award Agreement.

Any and/or all potential liabilities to ILDR with respect to a Grant and/or Award, etc., are to be based solely on any contractual obligations that may be created by THEIPLAN and/or an Award Agreement.

No Awards granted by NUBOE with respect to THEIPLAN shall be considered and/or deemed to be secured by any pledge on any WCOM and/or NUBOF property and/or any managed NUBOE property and/or asset, etc. At no time shall NUBOE, the Board and/or FUDR be required to give absolutely any security and/or bond for the performance of any obligation that may be created by THEIPLAN, Award and/or Grant, etc.

22. Important Plan Dates.

(a) Effective Date. The effective date of THEIPLAN is Tuesday, September 10th, 2024.

(b) Plan Termination. A majority of the Board may terminate THEIPLAN at any time with respect to any shares that are not then issued and/or linked to any Award, Option and/or Restricted Stock. Plan termination will not change and/or hinder any Awards already existing at the time of THEIPLAN Termination.

The undersigned, being the Acting CFO of NUBOE.COM, does hereby certify that the foregoing NUBOE.COM 2024 Incentive Stock Plan was approved by the Board of Directors and a controlling interest in NUBOE on Tuesday, September 10th, 2024.

Date

Alexander M. Perlaza, Acting CFO – NUBOE

pejiAds.com™

MotherlandMade™ .com .net .org

MotherlandMade.com™
Final Production: Africa

MotherLAN.Made.NET™
Leadership Africa Network

MotherlandMade.org™
Champions Aid Africa

Two Page View | Thumbnail View | Page Range: 50-51 / 201 | Guides

Ch 17 – 2025 SeeThreat.com MVP Complete | PejiAds.com & HoorooTu.com Underway

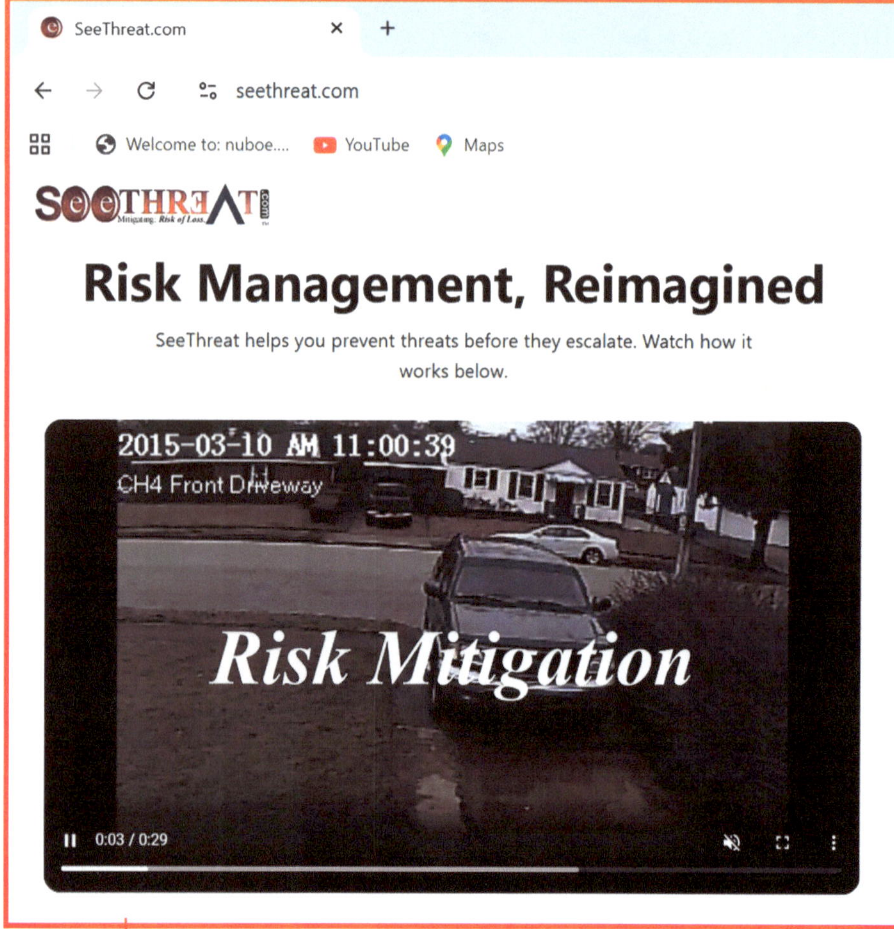

SeeThreat.com
seethreat.com
Welcome to: nuboe....
YouTube
Maps
All Bookmarks
Get Started
Risk Management, Reimagined
SeeThreat helps you prevent threats before they escalate. Watch how it works below.
2015-03-10 AM 11:00:39
CH4 Front Driveway
Risk Mitigation
0:03 / 0:29

We also completed MVP development on our most critical cyber security system / platform, SeeThreat.com™. This platform is important because it helps the ecosystem manage threats and risks – internally and externally!!

Pejiads
pejiads.com
Welcome to: nuboe....
YouTube
Maps
All Bookmarks
About Us
Contact Us
Log In
Sign Up
Broad Range. Tremendous Reach.
The purpose of this brand is to manage: all related network sponsorships, partnerships, technologies, systems, platforms, products, and services.

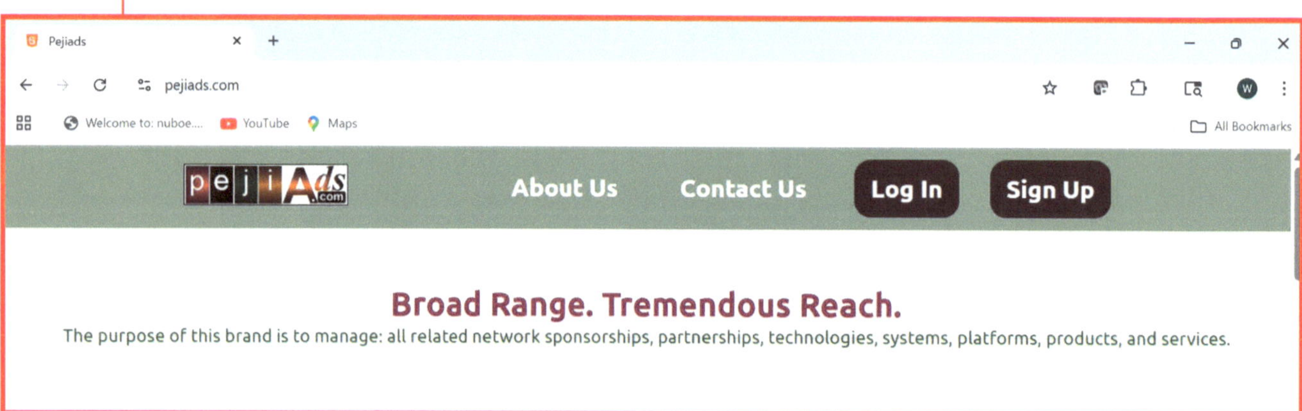

We also continued work on the **PejiAds.com™** ecosystem advertising and analytics system, and begun extensive work on the global country manager platform, **HoorooTu.com™**.

Ch 17 – 2025 The, "Hollywood," Global Talent Contract Commences

In 2025, we also began yet another critically IMPORTANT work. It's the global 360-talent management contract, which we'll use to sign on various live human talents and spokespeople, etc.

This work/book is nearly 90% (or more), exactly like, "Ground Floor," with the exception of an additional chapter at the end, "*360 Talent Management*" which spells out the terms and conditions of being aboard the ecosystem in an official talent / spokesperson role, etc.

(49) 2025 1st Class Jubilee trip to Rome

(50) 2025 Vatican St. Peter's Basilica

(51) 2025 TIME 100 Most Influential Companies Invitee

(52) 2026 WilliamMandela.com™ Global Boards Contract Begins

Chapter 18 ('25 to '26)

Origin Milestones

(53) 2026 Mar-a-Lago VIP Invitee

(54) 2026 1st City of Little Rock Invite

(55) 2026 Dr. Cornel West Meet Invite

(56) 2026 Next Level Restructuring

(57) 2026 Formation of the Apex Dream Team (February 16th)
Near Full MVP Completion on:
Initial lilroc.com™ starter mobile app
SeeThreat.com™ Security mobile app

Ch 18 – 2025 1st Class Jubilee Year trip to Rome from EWR

Ch 18 – 2025 1st Class Jubilee Year trip to Rome from EWR

In late 2025, we took another 1st Class International trip off over into the holy city of Rome. Wow, what a DREAM?! American carrier, United carried us and their EWR lounge and 1st Class flight were truly exceptional!! Thank you United!

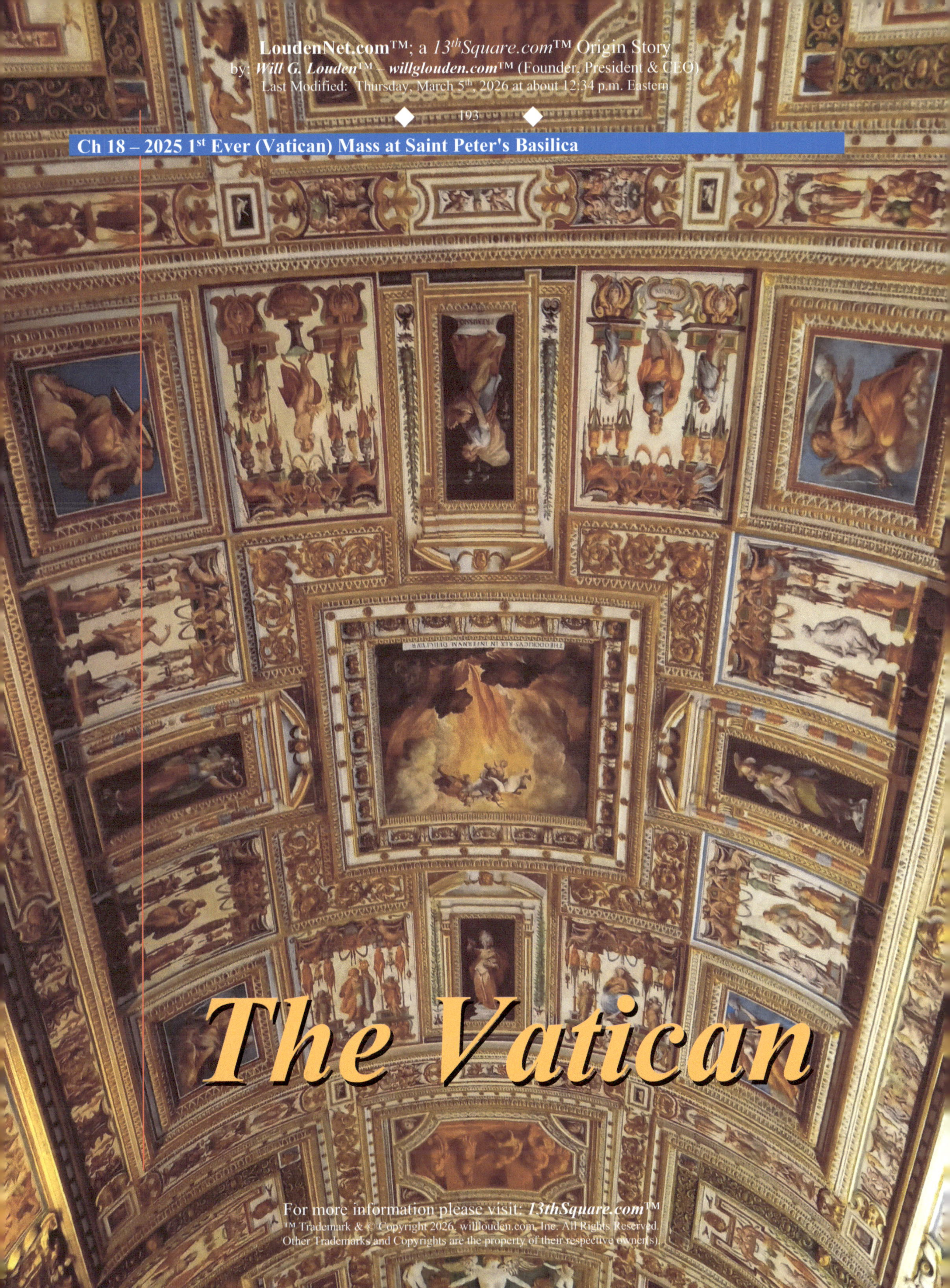
THEODORICVS REX IN INFERNVM DEIICITVR
The Vatican

Ch 18 – 2025 1st Ever (Vatican) Mass at Saint Peter's Basilica

Oh but that trip to the Vatican to attend one of the, "Pope Audiences," was also a true life TREAT. All things considered, Rome didn't disappoint.

Ch 18 – 2025 TIME 100 Most Influential Companies Invitee

TIME 100 MOST INFLUENTIAL COMPANIES

TIME100 MOST INFLUENTIAL COMPANIES OFFICE HOURS

Link shared upon RSVP

Monday, November 10 at 1:00pm

ABOUT

Since 2021, the TIME100 Most Influential companies list has recognized organizations shaping the future. Now, with the TIME100 Companies Impact Awards and the introduction of TIME100 Companies: Industry Leaders, the honors go beyond one iconic list.

Interested in learning more about how to make your entry stand out or how the judging process works? Join Emma Barker Bonomo, TIME Editorial Director, for office hours.

When we received the invitation from TIME Magazine to apply to become one of their 100 Most Influential Companies … The decision to look closer and attend an, invitation only, "Office Hours," was a, 'no-brainer.'

TIME 100 MOST INFLUENT!AL COMPANIES

Hi there,

I'm reaching out with a quick reminder about the upcoming office hours sessions for TIME100 Most Influential Companies.

These live Q&A's are your opportunity to get answers directly from TIME—whether you have questions about eligibility, category selection, what makes entries stand out, or the judging process.

Office Hour Sessions:

- Monday, November 10 @ 1PM ET

We can only host 25 participants per session, and spots are filling up quickly.

I look forward to seeing you there.

Best,
Emma Barker Bonomo
TIME Editorial Director

Ch 18 – 2026 WilliamMandela.com™ Book Start; Mar-a-Lago & Little Rock Invites

Hot out of Rome and right back home we started the year off right with several key milestones which included: (1) starting the global boards contract book, "William Mandela.com;" (2) 1st ever extremely welcomed invitation from the city of Little Rock; and (3) also an incredibly interesting exclusive invitation to do dinner at Mar-a-Lago too. wow!

City of Little Rock, AR - Government invited you to their event. Let them know if you can...

2026 further opened with a BANG with a truly amazing invitation to hear Dr. C. West speak at the Clinton Center along with the completion of several of our critical most MVP security systems, including: SeeThreat.com™. Substantial progress on many other foundational systems and platforms was also made.

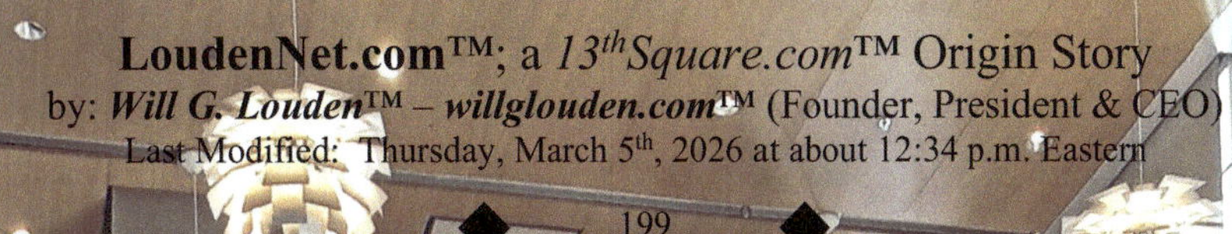

Ch 18 – 2026 The Apex Dream Team Formed and SeeThreat.com™ is Completed

Join us on **Saturday, January 31**, at **3 p.m.**, for the next installment of the Kumpuris Distinguished Lecture Series, "**Truth Matters: What Unites Us Despite Our Differences**," a conversation with **Professor Robert P. George** and **Dr. Cornel West.**

WY Secretary of State
FILED: 02/23/2026 05:45 PM
Original ID: 2024-001510600
Amendment ID: 2026-006397232

AMENDED AND RESTATED
ARTICLES OF AMENDMENT OF
NUBOE.COM
A Wyoming Corporation

The undersigned officers, directors, agents, and/or owners of NUBOE.COM, a Wyoming company (hereinafter the "Corporation"), for the purpose of amending and restating the Corporation's Articles of Incorporation as originally filed on, August 22nd, 2024, with an entity filing ID of: 2024-001510600, under the Wyoming Business Corporation Act, do hereby Amend and Restate the following Articles:

1. This Amendment to the Articles of Incorporation was adopted on, January 19th, 2026, by the NUBOE.COM Board of Directors; and

2. This Amendment to the Articles of Incorporation was also adopted on, January 19th, 2026, by the shareholders of NUBOE.COM; and

3. This Amendment to the Articles of Incorporation was also adopted on, January 19th, 2026, by the Controlling Stockholder of NUBOE.COM owning more than (eighty percent) 80% of all outstanding Capital Shares, entitled to vote at the time of this Amendment's adoption;

Received
JAN 27 2026
Secretary of State
Wyoming

1

Document ID: 269179bf-04ed-42a5-a2a2-ecc770f80604

In February of 2026, we formed THE Apex (Dream Team), and the state of Wyoming granted our requested, "Amendment with Restatement," to the NUBOE.COM, Articles of Incorporation. We made the decision to amend after a truly amazing hour long training with JP Morgan back in January of 2026.

Your Leadership Caught Our Attention – **Miami Titan 100** Opportunity

Hi Will,

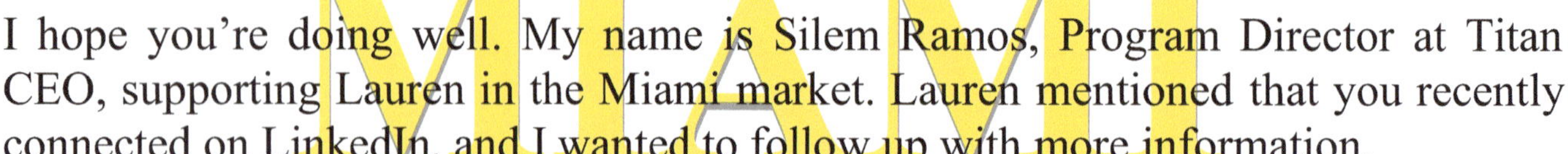

I hope you're doing well. My name is Silem Ramos, Program Director at Titan CEO, supporting Lauren in the Miami market. Lauren mentioned that you recently connected on LinkedIn, and I wanted to follow up with more information.

Based on that connection, we wanted to reach out and share more about the Miami Titan 100. Your leadership truly stands out, and we would love for you to be considered as part of our 2026 Miami Titan 100 cohort.

The Miami Titan 100 recognizes the area's top CEOs and C-level executives who demonstrate vision, passion, leadership, and influence in their field—100 Titans of Industry…

Howdy Silem Ramos:

Sincerest apologies for taking so long to get back to you…

Listen, this is a stunningly amazing and incredibly wonderful opportunity that under other circumstances I'd move Heaven and Earth to participate in and become apart of!!

Unfortunately, upon initial review I'm afraid to reply that we do not currently meet all of the application criteria (we do not make a mil a year and I don't live in Miami)…

Hi Will

Thank you so much for your thoughtful note and for taking the time to review the nomination opportunity—we truly appreciate it.

We completely understand your current criteria and appreciate your transparency. We'd love to stay connected and revisit this in the future if circumstances change and your organization aligns more closely with the program…

THANK YOU I LOVE YOU!!

Not the entire communications string. Some information has been omitted. (Initial email received: Apr 23 at 10:36 AM)

The '**origins**' of our "*phenomenal rise,*" to ***international stardom,*** maybe found within…

Come along with us, as we take you on an absolutely incredible journey and rise to a pathway filled with peace, joy, contacts and resources, which were/are priceless, and simply irreplaceable!! It's a distinctly Divine:

PURPOSE!

1997 VGIS Started
as Virtual GraphX, Inc.
1998 NWA Living™
2005 U of A Graduate
2006 1 on 1; WMT, CEO
2006 NWA Living TV
2007 willlouden.com™
2008 Hollywood VIP
2011 Eastern Europe
2012 willlouden.com, Inc.
2012 Obama Campaign
2013 20-Yr Class Chair
2014 Whole Home Reno.
2020 NJIT Capstone
2021 Dubai King Invitee
2021 First Visit to Africa
2022 Tanzania, Africa
2022 US Africa/US Trade
2022 Silicon Valley Visit
2024 Cape Town 1st Visit
2024 Mobile App Dev
Google and Apple Stores
2024 Botswana I Hub
2024 Moroccan King
Nigerian Weeding Invite
2024 Google Cloud Call

2024 NUBOE.COM Start
2024 Ground Floor Done
2024 JP Morgan Cap Tab
2024 Rite2Rule.com™
2024 Main Logos Locked
2024 Silicon Valley Trip2
FB | Google | Apple
2025 Trump Ball Invitee
2025 Nigeria, Africa Visit
2025 Pretoria Visit
2025 NUBOE Board
2025 PayPal Manhattan
2025 Byte Knights Start
2025 Ground Floor R2R
SeeThreat.com™ MVP
1st Class Jubilee to Rome
TIME 100 Invitee
Forbs Books Shoutout
2026 Mar-a-Lago Invitee
Little Rock City Invite
2026 Dr. Cornel West
2026 Apex Team Forms
Peachscore Accelerator
Who's Who in America
770+ Credit Score
Hall of Fame Invitee

International Hall of Fame Nomination – April 2026 Entrepreneurs' Diaries Recognition

Hall of FAME

Will, your decades of tech innovation just earned you a seat in Bangkok — Vanguard Impact Summit & Awards 2026 🏆

Visa Nominations <nominations@visawards.com> Apr 19 at 1:25 AM
To: @willlouden.com

Dear Will,

My name is Marcus Luke, and I sit on the Editorial Board of Entrepreneurs' Diaries, an invite-only publication built for leaders who have built something meaningful.

We don't reach out often. And when we do, it's because the profile in front of us has earned it.

Yours has.

Our research team monitors over 200 expressions of interest daily. From that pool, we narrow to 10–15 candidates per cycle. From those, our jury identifies 1–2 individuals worthy of direct contact. Will—you're one of them.

"After reviewing your work across Nuboe.com, MotherlandMade, AfricanParliament.com, and your broader body of work as an author and systems innovator, one thing is clear: you've been building quietly and meaningfully for a very long time. Most people don't recognise that kind of sustained, multi-decade entrepreneurship. We do."

Attending In Person? You're Our Guest.
Should you choose to join us in Bangkok, we've partnered exclusively with Novotel Bangkok Sukhumvit 20 to ensure your stay is taken care of — and you're welcome to bring one companion to share the experience:

- 4 Nights Luxury Accommodation for You + 1 Companion
- Daily Breakfast for Two
- Red Carpet Arrival & Gala Seating
- Closed-door Networking with Global Leaders
- Full-day Summit Access for You + 1 Companion
- Exclusive Networking Dinner

We hope to welcome you to Bangkok. Warm Regards MARCUS LUKE Editorial Board || Entrepreneurs' Diaries Vanguard Impact Summit & Awards 2026 ENTREPRENEURS' DIARIES || MONARCH FUSION CONCEPTS · UN COUNCIL || GLOBAL IMPACT LEADERSHIP SERIES

FAIR USE NOTICE

This book may contain, "marks," and/or copyrights belonging to other parties. In all cases where this may occur, all interests in those marks and/or "rights," etc. is hereby disclaimed, in their entirety, by the book author, publisher, and distributor(s), etc. etc.

In all situations where a mark and/or a copyright may appear, that does not belong to the literary work's creator, allowances are hereby made for, FAIR USE, and displayed solely for example, illustration, and/or educational purposes – ONLY.

FAIR USE NOTICE

Willintl.com™
First: Enjoy the Journey!
2026
UNITED
Polaris
We welcome international business class travelers departing to the following destinations:
• Africa
• Asia
• Europe
• Middle East
• Oceania: Australia, New Zealand, Tahiti
• South America: Argentina, Brazil, Chile, Peru
Customers departing to other international destinations in business class are welcome to visit a United Club℠ location.
Visit united.com/lounges for more details.
Thanks United!

www.ingramcontent.com/pod-product-compliance
Lightning Source LLC
LaVergne TN
LVHW070118110826
845147LV00002B/150

9781637624500